THE ULTIMATE REALITY

BOOK III

GIAN KUMAR

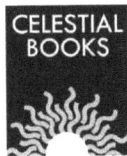

CELESTIAL BOOKS

ISBN 93-81836-89-7
© Gian Kumar, 2014
Cover: Deepanshu Rishi
Layouts: Ajay Shah
Printing: Dhote Offset Technokrafts Pvt. Ltd.

Published in India 2014 by
CELESTIAL BOOKS
An imprint of
LEADSTART PUBLISHING PVT LTD
Trade Centre, Level 1, Bandra Kurla Complex
Bandra (E), Mumbai 400 051, INDIA
T + 91 22 40700804   F +91 22 40700800
E info@leadstartcorp.com   W www.leadstartcorp.com
US Office Axis Corp, 7845 E Oakbrook Circle, Madison,
WI 53717, USA

TO ALL SPIRITUAL BEINGS.

About the Author

Gian Kumar was born into a traditional Hindu family, in Burma (Myanmar). From childhood, his life held paradoxes. While he was educated at a Christian boarding school, which observed strict religious practices, these were diametrically opposed to the Hindu traditions and customs that were the norm when he went home for the holidays.

A thinker by nature, the inherent confusion and dogmas underlying religion, gradually impelled him towards spirituality. Today, he is deeply grateful for a journey filled with opportunities to learn about existential riddles such as: *Who am I? What is my purpose in Life? Is God an illusion?* Gian hopes to share his own experiential learnings with others through the medium of his books.

Gian lives with his family in New Delhi. He can be reached at: giankumar@ymail.com

....

Book I   Know Thyself
Book II   Think From The Heart
          Love From The Mind
Book III The Ultimate Reality

Editor's Note

Repetitions, in the spiritual context, are unavoidable since the concepts are infinite while the words to describe them remain pitifully finite. In this series, the author has constantly used concepts and words such as the Absolute, Oneness, Energy, Self and so on. Besides, intellectually the author has considered the reader's need to understand and absorb the subject, step by step. Hence, the core ideas being repeated at each juncture, helps the message to be distilled and internalized, instead of remaining partially understood.

It does not necessarily follow that the reader agrees with everything written. When the mind becomes impatient or restless, signaling it has understood, the reader should move on. The subjects/chapters often revolve around just one word such as 'awareness' or 'oneness', which stands like the basic scale a classical raga is based on. Thereupon, a myriad variations and nuances are played, to attempt to convey the numerous extensions possible within the same theme.

The serious seeker of spiritualism in life returns by compulsion, to read repeatedly and hear those notes as a recurring melody, until the theme becomes clear. Like chanting a mantra, he then gains the proper perspective to practice what he has read.

CONTENTS

INTRODUCTION

Science defies God
Religion isolates God
Spiritualism sees God in all

SPIRITUALISM, IN ITS TRUE ESSENCE, is never attained by seeking; it cannot be bought off the shelf or found by listening to discourses on enlightenment or liberation. Spiritualism, unlike religion, is achieved purely through our way of living. It is an ongoing process in which the mind is set aside.

I am neither a spiritual teacher nor highly spiritual. In all humility, I am a seeker of fulfilment in life. My efforts at writing on this subject have led me to believe that spiritualism, like life, flows unconditionally – the more we know and comprehend, the more intriguing it becomes. The first two volumes of this set were on *self-knowledge* and *self-awareness*; now this third volume discusses *self-realization*, completing the spiritual story. This book provides methods, by which to reach totality and oneness in spiritual living, without any super-spiritual enlightenment.

Spiritualism has always been related to religion and mysticism. Today, however, science and spiritualism have come closer; physics, for example, besides its classical theories, has postulated new dimensions in the field of quantum mechanics, with respect to energy. These discoveries claim that all that is present in our universe is energy and that the creator and creation are one, changing our outlook towards God and religion, life and reality.

This series of three books explores the story of life in all its contemporary and scientific aspects, with respect to self-knowledge, consciousness and oneness, supported by ancient philosophies, thereby answering practically any question we may have about existence.

Life and death revolve in cycles. The dualities of pain and pleasure, rich and poor, happiness and sorrow will continue as parts of our existence. How to flow in that stream, maneuvering the mind, body and spirit, without condoning or renouncing anything, is the art of living we all hope to accomplish. An in-depth understanding of complex terms like 'awakening', 'liberation' or 'enlightenment', in the context of spiritualism, is addressed; not for the sake of seeking or desiring such philosophical terms, but to inculcate a state of knowing, experiencing and living with awareness, for the rest of our lives.

The body and mind, in spite of intellect and bodily comforts, remain separated until they finally unite with the cosmic spirit. The most important aspect of life is how to align these energies in the right manner – arriving at the point at which we can be at peace within ourselves. The universal spirit teaches us that we cannot live alone; there has to be a continuum and relationship with everything around us. Today, many of us feel there is something amiss, leaving us continually dejected and depressed, even at the zenith of our lives and careers. Overcoming this sense of vacuum requires a different approach, keeping in mind that we are born with, and live and die within, certain limitations.

The complex topic of life and its realities – dealing with science, spiritualism, religion and man – needs a fresh overview in terms of practical methods, where we become more human than divine and are not required to renounce anything. The emphasis is placed on strengthening our individuality rather than the guidance of priests or gurus.

The purpose of this book is to make us aware of material realization, through self-knowledge, self-realization and experiential living, knowing the unity and oneness of everything.

Many of us have no idea what enlightenment is, nor have we attained any awakening about or liberation from our miseries. Our sufferings and mental disturbances go on. The worst is we are neither aware of their causes nor are we overly concerned about them. In fact, most of us never realize that spiritualism needs neither to be taught nor sought; which is why so many seekers become dejected when their questions remain unanswered, unless of course, we blindly start believing what we are told. The spiritual methods we will read about here are more connected to fulfilment, peace and joy in life rather than how to realize enlightenment as achieved by only a few, such as Buddha or Jesus.

Whether my thoughts turn my readers into believers or not, I offer them the belief that, we are all one, in both our seeking and our ultimate reality...

The world is the river of God,
Flowing from Him and flowing back to Him.
On this ever-revolving wheel of being
The individual self goes round and round
Through life after life, believing itself
To be a separate creature, until
It sees its identity with the Lord of Love,
And attains immortality in the indivisible whole...
~ Upanishads

CHAPTER 1
PURPOSE OF THIS BOOK

THIS BOOK IS INTENDED FOR THOSE who have accepted their imperfections and seek to change. We may wish to improve but not to the extent of overloading ourselves with spiritual literature teaching us about consciousness and how to shed our egos, desires, etc. There has been much written on these subjects and yet we remain discontented and unhappy. Above all, immorality abounds and surrounds us.

Metaphysically, it is not for us to determine or judge all that our experiences have unfolded in life.

Being human is a divine gift. It is also not necessary that we overcome all our sins and become saints. We need to realize that we are born imperfect and will remain so until death. We are not here to prove to others that we are perfect. Moreover, we rarely come across anyone today, whether preacher or seeker, whom we can confidently declare to be spiritually enlightened. Whatever any guru, preacher or our own self may say, we can never give up our egos, material comforts, money or attachments, all of which we cherish. We are designed to live with our ego, dualities and separatism. Imagine a movie, which has no drama of love and hate, or a tale of only happiness where there are no challenges. How uninteresting or boring would that be! Yet, while accepting the way we are, can we work toward a better understanding of ourselves? While the imperfections will remain, it is only the degree to which we wish or are able to alter within ourselves, that can make us happier.

In this series, the first book, *Know Thyself*, dealt with Self-knowledge. How can any person transcend without first knowing the truth about his inner self? The second book has an interesting title: *Think from the Heart, Love from the Mind.* In it, I have emphasized how to go beyond knowledge towards the path of Self-awareness – awareness of our thoughts and the now, in expanding our consciousness, our spirit, beyond those external perceptual thoughts, where we begin to understand the importance of aligning the three elements of body, mind and spirit.

This third volume takes us on a journey beyond the mind – to what I call *The Ultimate Reality* – Which goes beyond knowledge, awareness and consciousness and all we can conceive or comprehend. I have delved into that which is existential – pure experience – where the mind has barely any role. I know this is a difficult topic and few have ventured deep into it, but I am making this attempt with strong conviction, backed by historical data from India. The concepts, however, have no allegiance to any one place or religion. They are based on logic, science and spiritualism, and whatever heights human intellect has achieved through the external and internal perceptions of the mind, rather than mysticism.

Wisdom comes when the heart connects to the mind. Whenever we see, feel and think from the heart, our whole perception changes. The heart normally used in this context, is more of a paraphrase of an emotional state. Heart, is an organ, purely meant to distribute blood all over our body; the real heart, in fact is in the mind. Whenever emotions affect the mind, our actions tend to be biased through our desires and attachments. However, the neural connection between the emotional mind and the heart is so strong that any hyperactivity in the mind, directly affects the heart.

Moreover, besides the mechanical heart, we have the mental heart, which bears all the emotions from our thoughts and memory. The third is the spiritual heart, connected to the soul. The first is the center for the body, second for the mind and the third is based on our intention and consciousness. When the mental or the spiritual heart opens, you feel the vibrations in the physical. They all exist side by side and we are to nourish them.

This book questions why, even with all the knowledge and awareness available to us from various preachers and gurus, we remain the same happy-unhappy souls, swaying about in doubt and restlessness. This in-depth study is based on the wisdom contained in the millennia-old *Upanishads*, which reveal that however high the consciousness may rise, unless we corroborate it with right action the mind alone cannot give the spirit solace.

The mind is designed to think exclusively of 'my' religion, country, name, family, friends and possessions. This is true irrespective of the fact that we may have gained some knowledge of self-development and raised the levels of our consciousness by learning yoga, meditation, etc. As long as we think from the mind, self-interest will continue to dominate all other factors.

Suppose one is a celebrity in the field of spiritualism, proclaiming and providing mental therapies to disciples; even then one is still prone to ego, boosted by one's cult following. The reason is that one is interested in spiritualism, more as a business and in creating a brand for oneself or the institution one belongs to. Eventually, a false sense of self prevails.

Under the influence of media, money and fame, all one cares about is oneself. Similarly, one would be right to assume that I too, under the influence of my ego, will need to do the same things to ensure the success of my books.

While we may become a bit wiser, we remain the same egoists, unless of course, we are inspired to sacrifice ourselves to the universe, and our deeds, speak for themselves. Mahatma Gandhi, Nelson Mandela and Mother Teresa were concerned with the good they did rather than in promoting their names and personalities.

Is there any other answer, beyond everything we know of the mind, body and soul, beyond awareness, consciousness and liberation? Is there a reality that goes beyond all teachings; one that cannot be preached or taught? We cannot stop the mind from doing its job of segregating, analyzing and dividing everything around, or from seeking wealth, comfort and materialism. No one has ever been able to do this; nor will any preacher ever succeed in doing so.

Why not take this opportunity to learn an Eastern philosophy, from the *Upanishads*, documented as scripture over 5000 years ago? *Upanishad* literally means 'to sit under a tree and listen to a spiritual master'. These are philosophical texts on the concepts of *karma* (action), *moksha* (liberation), *atman* (soul) and *brahman* (the all-pervasive absolute or single reality in the form of spirit or energy); they are the oldest testaments on spiritualism. The *Upanishads* emphasize oneness rather than separating the energies of our existence into dualities in a vicious cycle of pleasure and pain.

Why do we need to know or understand what it means to go beyond knowledge, awareness or consciousness? The reason given by these scriptures is that all things are connected within the mind, which can only function in dualities. The spirit or Self is clearly one and not two; there is no duality. Not only that, the spirit continues universally as one cosmic spirit, in one unified consciousness.

Science, in the field of quantum mechanics, is coming to the same conclusion and for that reason, the subject has been repeatedly referenced here. In duality, one gives rise to another; as from the whole, a portion is separated. Just as in the midst of lies, truth is born. Otherwise, there would be no way of knowing the truth. Absolute truth, however, is not a contradiction. If you consider God as absolute truth, no other god or devil can be related to Him. However, if the definition of the Devil did not exist in the mind, the need to define God would also be unnecessary.

Hence, both parts of any duality, in reality, are one. Being two sides of the same coin, each is intrinsic to the other. It is only the mind that causes a separation. Furthermore, the mind needs to be identified with its own *I*, to formulate its ego, based on the need to feel unique from all others. This is how our minds evolve from childhood; a child innocently cries to hold onto his toys, inadvertently forming his first attachments to material possessions. At a later stage in life, he finds that even the intangible wisdom of higher consciousness is not able to break the bond between tangible assets and one's self-esteem. This brings dualities into our lives, as well as a feeling of isolation from others.

We need to understand and seek the possibility of recourse from this madness within us. The ego, which is meant to be an instrument of our progress, eventually turns into our master. What can possibly go beyond all this, to a place where one need not give up on the mind's constant ticking of thoughts and still achieve the desired level of calm? The answer lies in entering into the no-mind zone as often as we can, as and when it pleases us. Here we learn the art of giving the mind a rest.

Once we slow down the functioning of the mind, even for a little while, it becomes a different mind altogether. Through its limited perceptions, the mind only sees a distorted and illusive reality; a reality which keeps changing as per our convenience, with every change in our thoughts. Like science, the mind is always in a state of doubt or suspicion, trying to impose its ideas on others. So we need to alter the basic concept of mind communion. Instead of external perceptual thinking, we should, at times, bring our minds to the point of intuitive thinking or inner perceptions, through pure experience. For example, love blossoms best when we are experiencing it, with the external mind playing no part. Love is one of the best ways to communicate, so long as it is not a part of duality.

In duality, the mind causes love to have expectations, which are bound to lead to hurt, since not all the parameters can be fulfilled at all times. This sort of conditional love gives birth to dislike, hurt and then hate. Even when making love, the mind can easily disturb the experience if we become distracted. It is only during orgasm that two bodies are in total unison, in the no-mind zone. In that particular moment there is no duality. The message during that exquisite moment is conveyed only in the language of the heart. It is love experienced as divine oneness, through pure surrender. There is no asking for the return of what one is giving or receiving. This sort of timeless period is referred to as a state of the Absolute or Oneness.

The Absolute is a state in which no thinking, intellect or mind is required. Only observing, knowing, experiencing and action come into play. This is why the mind, through the perceptions of the five senses, is limited to thoughts of duality, leading to discrimination and the conflict of choosing between this and that – primarily the result of self-centeredness. In the Absolute, there is no application of science, logic, intellect or separatism because it is purely experiential in totality and completeness.

In the same manner, imagine oneself mingling with the birds and bees, clouds, waves, crowds, machines, or anything else you come across; just observing, flowing and accepting the way it is. What peace and tranquility the whole experience will bring you. When your intuitive mind is in control, you are in a state of total awareness of nature and the environment, with the mind in silent mode, simply absorbing, acting and experiencing, rather than comparing, analyzing or judging. There are two stages in existence: one, to feel the presence of your own being, as part of the universe, in absolute oneness; and the other is to deal through your perceptive mind with the dualities of our materialistic world, for the sake of comforts, self and family. Imagine combining idealism and realism and merging the two into one. This is what I hope you will do as you read on.

Thus, it is only in knowing and understanding that the transformation within us can be created, not by thinking, learning or preaching a philosophy. When we think, we disturb the rhythm of knowing, for knowing is just to be or *let be*. Thinking is mainly for our own emotions, our personal *I* – directly or otherwise. Only in knowing, will our actions bring the required sensitivity to coexist in this universe in resonance with the oneness that encompasses, comprises, and composes all of us.

We all know that the most important factor in life is the force that makes us function. Our existence itself is comprised of this force called energy. One of the most significant discoveries of science is this force is all that there is – existing as indivisible, indestructible, pervading and permeating the whole universe. For over 5000 years, spiritualism has claimed exactly the same truth: that *brahman* (energy) exists everywhere, in the form of God, Spirit or Universal Consciousness.

Now, for this force to manifest as matter, or what seems to the eye to be solid mass, there has to be energy as gross in the form of body, subtle as the mind, and core as consciousness. In order for consciousness to express itself in an individual, it must experience through the laws of attraction and repulsion, by discriminating and choosing, in dichotomies and dualities. Duality is present in all of us, as male/female, God/Devil, positive/ negative, etc., separating the oneness of the existence into extremes. Consciousness differs in each individual, depending on the degree of one's own personal commonsense and level of awareness.

In this manner, the mind, through its perceptual reality, can only think in dualities. In order to balance the ambiguity of living with opposites, nature has provided us with the power to manifest pure, intuitive, intelligent energy in the form of awareness, to harmonize and purify ourselves through individual levels of consciousness. Thus, consciousness is the sole factor in determining what we really are.

*Truth, love and God are all the
same. For in them there is purity,
In us there is a separation of
dualities; happiness and sadness.*

Chapter 2
State of Higher Reality

THERE IS A CERTAIN MAGIC when we get down to doing something earnestly. When there is a strong urge to do something, we start dreaming, imagining, thinking and breathing about that subject. Mystically, divine forces converge in the mind to direct and guide us towards the goal. This happens when we start thinking from the heart, which cries for help, as a child does for his mother. We go beyond intellect or awareness when we become submerged in our subject night and day. Maybe that is why we are often told to sleep on a problem, and then the next morning we have our answer. It is probably the dissolved state of awareness doing its job in our subconscious. I may be writing mystically, but on a non-mystical subject. It is for the reader to judge whether there is logic in the pages that follow.

The ultimate path to self-realization, by whichever means we choose, will come back to the same point: that we all are interrelated, interdependent and interconnected, meaning we are inseparable. It is because we break this basic principle of life, separating ourselves, discriminating and making choices that we go through the roller-coaster ride of pleasure and pain. Living in oneness is in itself the highest form of self-realization, beyond any enlightenment or higher consciousness. It seems so simple. Even if we can imbibe just a fraction of this into our lives, we will not need any external guiding source. All we need to do is be the way we are and mingle with our environment with total acceptance and grace.

From time immemorial, there have been sages, preachers and gurus in various parts of the globe, yet none have been able, despite all the wealth of their experience and intellect, to make any headway towards improving society. In fact, our values have deteriorated from what they were even a decade ago. We may be more comfortable today in the lap of luxury and technology, but we are so self-centered that there is constant anxiety, discontent and unhappiness everywhere.

Most spiritual gurus today are concerned with improving our consciousness in order to rise toward divinity. To me, this is in itself a duality – going from unconsciousness to consciousness. Similarly, we are told that in our existence, bound in duality, there are bound to be extremes: God and Devil, good and bad, happiness and sadness – each an inseparable part of the other.

In such preachings too, there are shortcomings; otherwise there may not have been such an increase in immorality everywhere. Howsoever we may suppress our egos, improve our so-called inner self or consciousness, as long as duality remains, so will imperfection. We will keep swinging and swaying from one to another. These are bondages from which we cannot liberate ourselves.

Therefore, we may just be fooling ourselves by reading and listening to such spiritual enlightenment. Out of misery, some people make efforts to pursue spiritualism and seek enlightenment, thinking it will provide the answers. They feel dejected after a while, through a lack of understanding; not having realized yet that *there is nothing to seek*. To seek is to desire, which never provides permanent satisfaction. In desire we always remain wanderers, wanting more and more, never knowing where it will end.

My purpose in writing this book is not to enlighten, but to awaken people to this realization – that since everything in life is dual, you have no choice but to accept both roles in seeking external and inner wealth. However, wisdom can dawn if you become aware of what lies beyond this life of dualities: knowledge, awareness, consciousness, or something more perhaps? Methods of learning to achieve the right balance between the two extremes become necessary.

In simple words, these extremes of duality need to be brought closer to a meeting point, to the center from which they have broken off. It is mainly to improve upon who we really are and what we have become. What are the methods we should practice to bring oneself into balance? I have attempted to provide some here. Science and quantum mechanics have also tackled this subject, concluding that in the substratum of all that exists in this universe, there is only one constituent – energy.

I have asked many serious devotees the definition of spiritualism or spirit and they are inevitably surprised. They believe they will be awakened into enlightenment one day, and not only that, but in a jiffy! They still need to understand that even religion does not promise us magic. Perhaps all we can really expect it to do is convert us into believers. How can we then expect more from spiritualism, which is purely there to guide us through certain patterns of living in order to control the mind and its thoughts?

Firstly, religion provides a certain identity. Secondly, it is a belief or faith, whether right or wrong, which promises to take you towards God. Even though it may seem outdated, it does provide an Aspirin sort of relief temporarily, especially to disturbed and distressed minds. It also makes us feel humble when we bow our heads in the belief that there is someone superior to us. Religion on its own is sublime and spiritual. However, when attached to any culture, faith or society, it becomes separated with identification.

Religion probably came into existence from one of our primal emotions: fear. Our ancestors began bowing in fear towards volcanoes, clouds, mountain peaks and rivers. Later, when some strong or intelligent man out of the whole lot noticed this fact, perhaps he thought that if everyone could bow to clouds and mountains, why not to him?

So it continued, instilling one fear after another into the mind, with supernatural narrations and events and warnings that if people did not succumb to certain doctrines, they would be sinners and therefore doomed. Gradually, religions brought in rituals, traditions, fables, castes and creeds, all to alienate one from another. The basic essence, even today, lies in fearing God rather than loving Him.

Spiritualism is new to the Western world. In the middle ages, while the West was fighting its wars, the East was basking in the glories of wealth and peace. During that period, as recorded in scriptures dating back thousands of years, spiritualism was already in existence among the wealthy and powerful, so their spiritual leaders could make them even more prosperous. Today, despite the reverse, with the Western world far more developed, with all its wealth and technology, there still exists a need to understand the secrets of the East to satisfy a basic quest: how to silence the mind.

Most spiritual writers have delved deeply into various eastern philosophies, earning fame and tremendous wealth. They claim they know the path to attaining enlightenment, *moksha* and *nirvana*. Spiritualism, however, never promises enlightenment, dramatic awakening, or liberation from any bondage. It mainly provides methods of living as a fusion of mind, body and the beyond. The beyond is also referred to as consciousness, soul, or *atman*.

Neither religion nor spiritualism should be denigrated if they are unable to provide the results we desire. The ideals behind both are tremendous and full of godliness. Moreover, religion should not be left behind today. It has embraced many spiritual teachings and activities in its fold. We are the ones responsible for manipulating both religion and spiritualism for our personal, social, political and financial gain, leaving many to feel betrayed. It is important for every individual to understand what is best for him, to become aware, and learn to use his mind and its thought processes as an instrument, rather than allowing it to become the master.

After spending years seeking enlightenment, when devotees realize there is nothing to seek, they begin to understand the first lesson of spiritualism: *the answer to everything lies in this very moment, in the present.* It is the awareness of the presence of 'now' that draws our thoughts away from the past and future, beyond ego, and turns us into spiritual beings full of love and compassion.

It seems so simple and easy, even though the intellectual mind keeps harboring fears of the future, drawing on knowledge of the past, and missing the presence of now. Why? Because the moment you come into now, it ticks away into the past. Now is only a fleeting moment. The mind functions from past knowledge to seek something you perceive, converting it into thoughts for the future – this mental process takes time. When the mind captures now, it has already gone into the past, making space for a new now. Biologically and functionally, the mind takes time to understand. So let it be, let this be as it is. Go with the flow in life, not with the speed of time but in oneness with the grace of nature, living fully from moment to moment.

Imagine sitting on the bank of a beautiful river, admiring the sheer beauty of nature. Your presence in that moment stretches. You become so involved in the beauty around you that you are mesmerized, losing your sense of time. This realization is far higher than any enlightenment. It can last as long as the mind does not interfere to distract you. If it does, everything vanishes into thin air. You start to compare, judge and evaluate the beauty before you. Submerging yourself in the moment can only happen when you are in total oneness with the universe.

Reduce your thinking by controlling your mind. Only then will you be able to appreciate every moment and the presence of yourself amidst all beings. You will also be able to understand what follows from being in the now – the state of oneness explained philosophically, scientifically and spiritually. The presence of oneness is not something you seek externally, for it lies within, where preachings and teachings have no significance.

Do remember, whatever success or greatness we may achieve in life through fame or fortune, as long as our body, mind and spirit are not aligned, we are bound to feel lonely and discontented, even at the top. There will be diminishing energy levels due to negative influences. A separation or gap in the three will never allow us to feel fulfilled in life. So what is the answer? To me, enlightenment is an ideal, a dream for the select few. I seek, like any other person, a peaceful life, mental contentment, material comforts and good health. These pages tell you how to achieve these through methods that align mind, body and soul. I ask you to make an effort, because that is all it takes, nothing more.

Our whole life is spent segregating and dividing, existing within opposites, swaying this way or that. We choose, dissect and analyze all that we come across – our likes and dislikes, our unending desires, sentiments and attachments, isolating *us* into *me* and *mine*. It means we are doomed to imperfection, self-destruction, greed, jealousy and immorality. Today we live in a society in which passions for materialism, wealth and promiscuity flourish. We are a part of a society which none of us, in our hearts, are ready to give up, but nor are we prepared to truthfully admit to condoning these anomalies.

We were taught in school that the most important elements of our existence are food, clothing and shelter; after that come wealth and fame; and only then comes self-actualization. However, the last should be our purpose in life, for fulfilment in every aspect.

Otherwise life remains a cosmic joke, revolving round and round in body-mind consciousness without ever reaching the higher consciousness of finding out who we really are. Righteously try to achieve economic progress to fulfil your desires so you think of going beyond, into *moksha* or liberation.

The lonely, separated spirit will keep calling,
Life will remain lonely, sad and discontented,
In spite of acquired wealth, comfort and knowledge.
You will remain ignorant and incomplete,
For illness of mind and body are because of your selfishness.

CHAPTER 3
THE LONELY SELF

IN ANCIENT TIMES, A PERSON seeking the spiritual path only had his guru to guide him. Without recourse to books, people went to *ashrama*s or spiritual centers to understand the complexities of the mind. Today, we have access to philosophies from all over the world, thousands of books, the Internet, and specialized new-age gurus. There is so much information available. Even so, things are not as they should be. People are still ignorant, and eager to know the ultimate answer to the riddles of life: Who am I? Who is God? What are we? How can we improve our lives and be peaceful and happy?

We, as seekers of such answers, are not serious in that endeavor if we cannot imagine parting with any of our material comforts or the fantasies of our egos; nor are our minds, even if we wished to give up these things, designed in such a manner. Today's spiritual gurus and writers, in my opinion, are involved in a futile campaign. We collect in large numbers to listen to some preacher, but mainly for social status or to network and further inflate our egos; all the time presuming we are becoming wiser. The lure of our illusionary world is too strong for anyone to be spiritually awakened, liberated or enlightened easily. In spite of all the effort, time and money spent, we cannot find any messiah enlightened enough to lead and guide us to spiritual awakening.

The same gurus, through their preachings and writings, gradually become more involved in establishing their businesses, centered on spiritual materialism rather than on trying to solve the human dilemma. We can see this in their branding, cultivated images, robes, hypnotic voices, and participation in media coverage regarding their personae or institutions. Thousands or millions are preached to and entertained, lured by the promise that if they follow the guru's techniques, the ultimate answer to life and enlightenment will be attained. But, even after all that, our false self or ego keeps raging like a tiger on the loose.

My philosophy neither speaks of such enlightenment nor does it give fodder to the intellect in an attempt to seek miracles. I simply convey a totality in life, pure existence in oneness, in which we are free and strong enough to lead our own lives in the manner that befits us. This is bound to give joy and strength in solitude rather than loneliness.

Everything I present here revolves around the concept and vision of oneness, its significance, and why we need to understand the basic law of nature. The concepts are simple to understand but difficult to follow, as we are all submerged in our own separate identities of self-interest and ego, gradually making us narrow, separate and isolated. I outline methods in a framework of how we should act in our day-to-day lives to achieve a certain balance, and thus experience the purity and meditative benefits of those actions.

My attempt is to draw away from a lonely, self-centered identity, explaining how the basis of reality has been separated from our limited perceptions and totality. How everything is so interrelated; that we are interdependent within our surroundings. This will give meaning to life with the ultimate reality revealed in its true identity.

Today, science tells us of the presence of such a unifying force. However, that force may dissect, analyze, change or separate from one form into another, the result of all physical matter is energy, which can neither be created nor destroyed. It exists in infinity and eternity, in a grid of unified consciousness, making each form dependent on another, thus signifying a creator/creation relationship.

This energy has no parameters; it is complete in itself, manifesting in different forms, leaping and sparking in dual properties of particles and waves, in pure harmony. We can merely disturb these movements, frequencies and vibrations by separating them through the dualities of human existence. The vicious dual cycle of good and bad will remain. However, while understanding the basis of our origin, scientifically and spiritually, I will divulge how to balance our multidimensional energies toward seeking fulfilment.

Science and spiritualism complement one another; indeed, a lot of scientific research starts with mysticism. The approaches are different. When a scientist studies a flower, he first tears it into pieces and identifies each part of its objective structure. He then gives a name and a function to each piece, and goes on to explain how pollination and cross-pollination work in its reproduction, and so on. However, he is never able to go beyond, to reach its beauty.

Spiritualism, on the other hand, subjectively goes deeply into the flower's fragrance and beauty, to reveal the completeness of its existence. Or it elaborates on how a seed from the flower, though complete in itself, flourishes to produce many more seeds, never finishing its cycle of existence, yet always remaining complete in it.

Science often requires spiritualism; otherwise, man and science will keep wandering and observing externally, seeking perfection. It is only when man goes within his inner self, uniting the objective reality of what he perceives with his subjective inner awareness, that he is able to complete his search for fulfilment. Both external and internal realities are part of one another and the same whole, yet they remain separate until they fulfil their purpose to become complete and absolute. This complex topic will be dealt with later in detail.

While expressing this universal phenomenon of oneness, some technical terms have been taken for granted, presuming that this is not the first book you have read on spiritualism. In addition, there will be repetition of some themes, which is unavoidable.

Perfection is a form of insecurity, a fear that we crave in order to satisfy our ego, trying to prove to others how superior we are. We need to face reality: we are imperfect, and will remain so. Our aim in life should be to create the right balance and cohesion between any polarities or dualities in which we exist, making efforts to bring them closer towards their center. It is only when we achieve this that we come closer to that ultimate perfection referred to as oneness, where there is no ego, only love and acceptance.

Being in a state of oneness is like the cohesion and harmony seen between planets or galaxies of stars, moving eternally in the universe. Life is like a river in which we all flow, with dualities on either bank.

The art of spiritual living lies in how, like the water, we are able to embrace, balance, accept and realize the two as one.

This perfection of being was seen and referred to by the sages of ancient times, as the universe being a single, eternal flow of *brahmn*, indivisible and indestructible, forever dancing and leaping. To them, all that existed was *brahman*, spirit or energy, in the form of God. Now, in the 21st century, nuclear physicists have noticed the same dance of the cosmic god Shiva in subatomic particles and waves. These particles, when they collide with the Higgs field, create mass. In a similar manner, modern science perceives matter not as solid form but as energy, in patterns of waves and particles, vibrating and dancing to perfection.

Eminent scholars like Carl Sagan and Fritjof Capra, have admired and often referred to this dance of

Shiva, projecting the personification of this eternal dance as creation and decomposition in our cycle of birth and death, identical to the eternal vibration in our subatomic zone. This thought has now matured to become the basis of the natural phenomenon of our existence in totality. Perhaps that is why a statue of Nataraj (Shiva as the cosmic dancer), stands in the CERN compound in Geneva.

Scientists are now telling us what was said thousands of years ago: that God is present in every particle of the universe, held in a creator-creation relationship. We are all a part of this creation, existing in separation due to our dualities, concerned externally with our self-centered lives, and so remaining lonely and imperfect. The creator keeps dancing eternally in completeness and absolute awareness, indestructible, telling us our ultimate fate lies in our physical destruction and decomposition, in order to become one with him.

The story of the cosmic god Shiva also tells us that the creator of the cosmos, Brahma (the energy provider), prayed and bowed before Shiva, pleading with him to grant an existence in which creatures could multiply and increase. Shiva, the absolute, who was always conjoined as one, male and female in one complete whole, had to separate into two opposites to exist and allow repeated cycles of birth and death for life to continue in eternity. With this came the power of discrimination and choice in the separated self, and the desire of how and in what manner to exist.

Thus, one became separated into two, entailing the illusion/delusion of our existence; for the two originated from one and went back to become one. In this way, in the cycle of birth and death, the physical body decomposes and goes back into the earth, but the core energy – the soul, atman, spirit – merges with the unified consciousness to restart and transmigrate into a new birth, and so continues life.

The Buddha seemed to differ in his philosophy. He remained silent about the soul, self, spirit or atman. This indicates the Buddha believed there is no continuation of the self, only one cycle of birth and death.

Due to this separation of absolute energy into dualities, despite being a part of the whole, the self remains lonely, ignorant, unfulfilled and imperfect.

This goes from one existence to another, in repeated cycles of birth and death, until Self-realization, when we rejoin the web of unified consciousness in total awareness and pure consciousness. In such a manner, Buddha, Jesus and a few others, realized enlightenment, not in separation, but in selflessness, compassion and devotion towards that oneness, to remain eternal in their own uniqueness.

What is the spiritual connotation of all this? Existence may end, but life continues its journey in repeated cycles of birth and death until it finally realizes eternity and immortality in absoluteness.

In spiritual living, we need to accept life in its totality, both negative and positive. We must outgrow our negativities in a natural manner, not by rejection in the mind but by transformation through acceptance of their totality and oneness. Here the mind plays a role only in observation and awareness, as an instrument, not interfering in any way to separate this totality for selfish ends. Remember that problems and conflicts in life are due to our being selfish and concerned only with ourselves, creating anxiety within and without. This life is as it is; let it be; merge with the whole to become one. In this way we become aware of our consciousness; we begin to understand the simplicity behind reality, without allowing our thoughts to enter into dualities, which disturb the oneness of life.

Our life is a play in the arena of the divine. We are those immortal souls, provided with physical existence to experience both pleasure and pain. We are here to live and experience different realities with our own share of conflicts and challenges. Existence was never meant to be easy nor is it ever going to be. We need to know, experience and understand individually through our own grit how to handle any situation whether in darkness or in light. We need to overcome all those challenges, which we face not with excuses but with answers. Therefore, how we face our dualities in life, both happiness and sadness is the art of living, which I wish to share.

What we need to remember or ponder upon is that the mind is an electrochemical processor of data, processing from both internal and external environments simultaneously. Thoughts in the sub-conscious, through our mental framework, are the hard disks, with data supplied by our senses, creating self-images. Most of the time these self-images are imaginary, but in our self-interest we start depending on them. They impose their will on our minds by taking control of our thoughts, memories, emotions, intentions and ambitions for the future, thriving on past-future dreams, in a realm where space, time and circumstance are constantly changing. Such factors definitely cannot be taken as reality. They make us reach vague conclusions about others, and ourselves purely in self-interest, placing our whole body and mind at the mercy of our emotions, discarding the truth and reality of any subject.

We then separate into an apparent or perceived reality of our own world, with self-made conclusions about who and what we are, what others are, and how we should relate to them. Thus we assume we are never wrong. This all-knowing 'rightness', leads to confusion, giving distorted results, purely for the sake of our false self, taking us away from that oneness of our real presence and being.

In the gap between what you are and what you can be,
Is your personal power telling you what you want to be.

CHAPTER 4
THE SPIRIT OF AWARENESS

IMAGINE COMING ACROSS A BEAUTIFUL painting or on a lovely sunset beach. Our awareness spontaneously captures such beauty and says, 'Wow!' without having time to think about it.

Later, however, when the mind becomes involved, the beauty is analyzed. The mind starts thinking and separating, comparing and choosing, deciding whether this is better or worse than something you have seen before.

In my second book, '*Think from the Heart, Love from the Mind,*' you will read that it is simpler to connect with our deeper self subjectively rather than through complex thoughts, which keep changing with differing circumstances. The idea is simple: there should be less separation into this and that, between you and me. Deep down, we share the same presence of one consciousness. You may need to read this chapter more than once in order to grasp the depth behind every statement and contemplate on the same. Today, in our complex world, simple things are the most difficult to fathom.

The presence of our being is very simple, absolute and one, it is the mind which is complex. Very much like an onion, it has layers of conditioning that we cannot see. Whatever, reaches the mind is either borrowed from others or corrupted through falsification by emotions, beliefs, ideology or society. For this reason, you require spiritualism to peel off those external buffers and penetrate inwards towards the center, our soul. Then the last peel is left, and there is nothing more but emptiness, your true and simple being. However, do you wish that? In theory, yes, but in practicality you would rather like to unwind the paradox of life and enjoy existence.

If everything was neutral, imagine there would be neither joy nor sorrow. That is why paradoxes are necessary; both need to be experienced in separation. Only then do we become aware of the other. It is awareness, which enlightens us to know, experience and realize the separation that we live in and become conscious of the same.

There was a woman, who was very knowledgeable. She became hooked to that knowledge and continued to accumulate more and more, being convinced that this was all there is to it. Not realizing that by knowledge, you may become a great scholar, writer or orator but not a knower.

With knowledge, you become an imitator and may feel you have understood. She imagined she knew all, but her inner state was that of confusion. Mind of a human is a paradox, and this mind is not what He is. His one leg is in materialism under ego and the other in spiritualism. The greatness is of that person, who without shunning or renouncing, lives with both, the material and beyond. For, the absolute content is in both, until we realize that the only way for peace and tranquility is through surrender, acceptance and gratitude.

Always remember, understanding is more out of experience than mere accumulation of knowledge. Like knowing God is existential and experiential, and not by scriptures alone. Your belief or faith is not going to change this reality. That is why, spiritualism may be referred to as mystical by its scriptures, but in reality while experiencing, it becomes a science. It does not believe on knowledgeable proof, it requires proof by experimentation and action in awareness.

In this volume, we venture to the point when consciousness awakens us to what and who we are; not only through the filter of our minds but also through experience. Existing as a part of this whole, from which we are separate, we try to achieve totality, surrendering and accepting all our actions, good or bad. Here, surrender is not to anyone but to oneself, in humility.

Moreover, to be mentally stable and physically healthy, one needs to possess, I have always believed, a strong, personal power. Though inherent, this power can also be developed through awareness and determination. Those with strong personal power have a greater understanding of the quality and betterment, possible in life, as compared to those who do not. Personal power, explained in detail in Book II, is about aligning intellect and spirit in the best manner possible. It comprises both a sound body (health) and a sound mind (intellect), in the spirit of awareness.

If awareness is necessary to our witnessing self, our power of reasoning (or for that matter our individuality or intellect), is equally important. Reason supports personal power not to be dependent on any external force beyond the body and mind. Our power of reasoning invites awareness to radiate into wisdom. Awareness or consciousness would be of no value without that power to reason. Deep down, awareness, consciousness and intellect are superimposed by thoughts, as they can be defined only by thoughts. However, the purity of our individuality or personal power is also developed by experiential realization, when thoughts alone cannot capture its totality. Our body and mind may decompose, but our individuality leaves its own imprint on the soul, to transmigrate further.

A person weak in personal power is gullible, believing in external sources and depending on outer beliefs and dogmas. His fears and anxieties can be temporarily suppressed by anyone intellectually stronger but he is bound to become a victim of religious, spiritual or organized institutions. He will be influenced by others' experiences, impressed by their strong personalities, and presume they are helping him to gain whatever he is seeking. Such a person is, in fact, giving up his freedom by falling blindly under the spell of supernatural or mystical narrations or traditional beliefs.

Most new-age gurus claim that following their tenets enable us to abandon ego, live in the now, and awaken our inner self to bliss. How easy it sounds! Nevertheless, do remember, no spiritual living is possible without personal freedom. This is the reason one should use one's mind only as an instrument, to collect and analyze data from knowledge obtained. Become mature, wise through experience, and knowing; be aware of every moment. To be strong, accept any situation, good or bad, and experience it – beyond thoughts, in the presence of awareness of who you are.

All this is incredibly simple, therefore it cannot be preached; it just needs to be experienced in silence, with minimum interference from the mind. The reason is that such simplicity of oneness evolves from selflessness rather than anything else. It transforms into compassion. All this is achieved in action and experience, rather than thinking with the mind. Even in cases of selfless action, when the mind interferes, it dilutes the whole process; the act becomes more about doing it to inflate our own ego than to merge with the oneness of all. Similarly, bragging about a charitable act inflates ego. The concept of oneness is simple, though our minds make it complex. It needs to be practiced in humility, which of course, is difficult. However, if practiced using the meditative methods explained later, it is sure to bring the required balance to attain fulfilment in our lives.

Spiritualism claims that our awareness is the context and sum total of our consciousness, meaning our sense of presence, as well as being alert from one moment to another, is the ultimate answer to wholesome living. However, in day-to-day living, the mind and intellect function as the sum total of the past, present and future. The mind, from its past, also projecting into the future, tackles any present situation in a composite manner.

According to new-age spiritual gurus, we should live in the now, not allowing thoughts of the past or the future to interfere in our lives. That means we are nothing physically, mentally we remain an optical illusion, and emotionally we cannot rely on the past or future. Thus, in normal existence, we are hemmed in from all sides.

I understand what quantum physics tells us about everything in this universe being energy. When we break any physical form down to its subatomic level, there is only energy. Or as Albert Einstein put it: 'A human being is a part of a whole, called by us *universe*, a part limited in time and space. He experiences himself, his thoughts and feelings as something separated from the rest...a kind of optical delusion of his consciousness.' This means we exist in an illusion of separateness, in our personal worlds of me and mine.

The question here is what the average person should believe and follow. This dilemma is probably the reason, being utterly confused, that most of us eventually fall prey to fanaticism, mysticism, caste, culture, creed and supernatural beliefs. With enlightenment being a distant dream, we remain lonely, anxious and discontented. Whatever we are, the most important thing is to know in simple and practical terms how one should tackle the complexities of life.

Would you not agree that if the answer was that easy, there would be bliss pervading the whole universe? Is it simplicity in life that we need to follow? But our minds with their never-ending desires, fears and insecurities, restrict that simplicity. Our ancient scriptures have given us brilliant answers, while science today is still unravelling the mystery behind the ultimate reality of who and what we are.

The *Upanishads* are unique; they are universal and bound to no particular religion. God is in creation itself in purity and total awareness pervading all there is in the universe. Here, God is distinguished as pure consciousness. For this reason, one may consider any form of energy as God, so long as the same is considered in total awareness or pure consciousness.

Accordingly, God is within us but remains dormant because of our separation into dualities; revealing Himself when we reach the stage of total awareness.

The knowledge of the *Upanishads* is as relevant today as it ever was thousands of years ago. It does not try to impose any supernatural beliefs based on transcendental reality; instead, it goes beyond rituals and what our senses perceive. It relies more on personal knowing, doing, living and experiencing. Any particular sage did not write these intense spiritual narrations but consist of collective wisdom, dictated by many; none of them wished for credit. They only sought to be a part of the reality we all belong to.

They strongly expounded on the single center of power, energy and reality, called *Brahman* or universe, which manifested in all creations, but transcended them as the single absolute source. They claimed that this reality is our real self, present in all of us, and sustains the universe. There is a framework or web, a unified force of interconnectedness and interdependence within our psychic energy, in the form of consciousness, which can be realized only through love and compassion. Individual consciousness, existing separately, within its limited space and time, can only come out of its misery and underlying fears when it becomes selfless and merges back into oneness, accepting the reality that we are all one.

These are also the basic principles referred to in *The Perennial Philosophy* by Aldous Huxley, as well as the new translation of *The Upanishads* by Alistair Shearer and Peter Russell.

The Upanishads are the oldest and clearest expression of the perennial philosophy that is the inner core of all great religions. Passed down by word of mouth for thousands of years, the Upanishads teach of an absolute and unified field of intelligence that underlies and permeates all creation. This divine ground is our nature, and to bring our lives into conscious harmony with it is the ultimate purpose of human existence.

It is time for us to learn the mysteries of Mother Nature; to understand and experience in what way our dual selves can connect with our absolute energy in togetherness, rather than remaining so much in separation into dualities. This is the secret behind the journey from subatomic waves and particles to the cosmos.

Quantum physics is of the same opinion, claiming all that exists in this world is nothing but energy, which is omnipresent, omniscient and omnipotent. We are an electromagnetic field, starting from the subatomic level to cellular, then physical form comprising gross, subtle, core and spatial energy. We are tied together in a field of spirit, manifesting as awareness, which, on merging with an individual's mind in his self-identity, turns into thoughts.

Further, when this overall energy is disturbed physically or psychologically, the *chakra*s or energy centers in our body, are no longer aligned in their frequencies and vibrations, reflecting as symptoms or ailments. Similarly, in metaphysics we are told that there is no separate reality of the individual. All of us are part of the same network or web of life, which is beyond anything we can perceive, permeate or penetrate. The experience of a separate self is just an illusion. Therefore, science has to delve deeper still and travel beyond its normal dissection of forms, to the realm of quantum consciousness, in order to discover the salient features and benefits of acceptance in totality with regard to oneness.

During my research on the subject, I came across this relevant quote by Albert Einstein (as mentioned earlier) that truly defines the essence of this book:

A human being is a part of the whole called by us 'the universe', a part limited in time and space. He experiences himself, his thoughts and feelings, as something separate from the rest – a kind of optical illusion of consciousness. This delusion is a kind of prison for us, restricting us to our personal desires and affection for a few persons nearest to us. Our task must be to free ourselves from this prison by widening the circle of understanding and compassion, to embrace all living creatures and the whole of nature in its beauty.

With the birth of quantum physics, both science and spirituality have come closer. Science is also deeply pondering the factor of nothingness: whether our universe is really comprised of something or is just energy; whether we came from something or nothing. I offered an elaborate elucidation, 'Power of Zero', in Book II. The *Upanishads*, of course, are very clear in declaring that existence is born from non-existence.

Imagine a void being the source of all creation. Visualize a tiny seed that seems to be nothing, yet gives rise to a huge tree, or a spoonful of salt that occupies space but disappears on dissolving into water. We perceive air as nothing but we can feel the pressure of its power when it blows against us; it must have some energy. There are innumerable examples of nothingness, like the humming of a bird or the radiance of the sun.

Therefore, what we see as images are superimposed projections of our perceptions, which differ from one living creature to another. This is explained in the *Upanishads*; it is only the spirit that pervades everything, not adhering to any time or space, silently flowing in its intelligence, as core energy, in the heart of everything. In order to discover this secret, one must experience this spirit, but only when the mind is detached from external perceptions and we witness the same through observation and awareness.

We come from nothing and go back into nothing;
That nothing is something,
that something is everything;
That everything is the cosmos.
Is this a grand joke telling us
Who we really are…just nothing?

CHAPTER 5
WHO ARE WE?

QUANTUM PHYSICISTS HAVE SHATTERED our egos, claiming that all the objects we see, feel and touch are formless in their subatomic state. Observing through very powerful microscopes, we see waves and particles of energy leaping and sparking simultaneously in dual fashion, in continuum, with everything existing on earth. These waves connect us to a serene, spaceless, timeless cosmos, flowing eternally. According to physicists, this is everything and all that we have. It is what we really are.

Similarly, from the oldest writings on spiritualism ever discovered, the source for Jainism, Buddhism, and Taoism, we learn all that exists in this universe is nothing but *Brahman* or spirit, pervading everything that there is. The creator is also a part of his own creation, part of the complete whole.

Besides that, the mind and our existence are nothing but a veil of delusion called *Maya*, just reflections of a grand phenomenon called life. We live in a misconception, thriving on an objective, apparent reality that is constantly changing and disappearing, which succeeds in creating a separation between us and the overall completeness all around us. The real you, the subjective self within – formless, infinite and eternal, in the form of intelligent energy or spirit, transmigrates from one life into another, from one birth to the next, until it reaches salvation in oneness with all.

This philosophy of *Advaita* in the *Upanishad*s admits only one existence, one reality, which is total and self-contained, thereby strongly negating existence in duality. The Buddha's philosophy differs in saying this reality is nothing but *shunya*, meaning empty – in which we eventually, upon dying, turn into emptiness. However, *Advaita* contradicts this emptiness, and leads us further to the concept of the Absolute God or *Brahman*, as non-destructible and eternal.

It explains that we are all a part of the same cosmos. After our bodies decompose, our souls, with the core intelligence-carrying energy, transmigrate into new bodies, as a part of that whole, on the premise that it can neither be created nor destroyed. In other words, we are all reflections of the same Supreme Reality or energy, manifested in different forms, dual in nature and so continuing this cycle of birth and death. Through these innumerable cycles of birth and death, life continues until we reach that final stage, where we become absolute or God, achieved by a few like Buddha and Jesus.

Ancient seers have defined three stages of advancement in such a reality. The first stage, which occurred in those times but no longer does, was to live entirely with nature, instinctively. Psychic energy, in this case, remains in close relation to nature, rather than being apart from thoughts of the mind. This is how animals live: in spontaneous awareness, where there is no discrimination or choices about this or that.

The second stage was existing in dualities, where the mind played the main role, thinking and evolving. So much is attributed to this stage that great philosophers like Descartes declared: *I think, therefore I am*, which was later amended by Jean Paul Sartre saying: *The consciousness that says I am is not the consciousness that thinks*. He discovered a new dimension in thinking but was unable to go beyond it.

The mind being supreme, all progress in this world has been attributed to this second stage. Here, thoughts flow like a river; one thought being replaced by another, and it keeps changing. Since thoughts are impermanent, it is postulated that the mind too, cannot be constant. The mind is seen here as limited to its body and self-consciousness, always requiring identification that is deeply connected to its past and future. All basic structures are formed in relation to this past and future, and influence the present. We start living more in those thoughts than in the moment.

But reality, even if it is apparent, always happens in the now. Truth or reality, when related to past or future has no relevance, as truth exists only in the present. Likewise reality; both tend to be changed by the personal thoughts of any individual. That is why reality or truth in the perception stage is considered illusionary or limited. Here, the biggest gift for existence is the awareness of the mind, whether connected to the past, present or future; permeating through as intelligent energy, keeping a check on our conscious thoughts and making us realize our real true selves.

The third stage is what the *Upanishads* are all about: spiritualism in which one goes beyond the mind. The Western world has dissected the mind into three: the conscious, the sub-conscious and the unconscious. In this *Upanishad* stage, to go beyond the mind or even to a no-mind zone, one achieves super consciousness, where the real self becomes a witness to the ego or mind. Spiritual gurus claim:

'You are what you are, when you do not think,' meaning that you rise from the level of 'I am' to 'I am that' – where man and spirit become the same identity and permeate the universe.

This stage is experiential realization, because the body, mind and spirit are all in a state of oneness, with no ego-consciousness; as a whole, in union with cosmic energy. I would say that what we experience happens in the now, but the mind cannot capture that now. So it is beyond the mind to narrate any experience accurately. Moreover, when more than one person is involved in an experience, each will have a different version of it. Experiences are the sum total of our individuality. It is us in totality – which the mind cannot capture. Spiritualism relies more on experience than on the mind. The mind is designed mainly to further our self-interests, which then cause conflicts; while spiritualism is designed to draw us away from the mind, into experiential realization, to show us how we are all one and the same.

In Spiritualism, the three stages of reality are clearly defined: illusionary, empirical and the absolute. In spiritualism, you need to fall first to rise; you need that knowledge of the Self. Then comes the experiential through awareness. Last, though not possible by normal living is that of the absolute, pure consciousness in total awareness with Self-realization.

In the initial stages when you are acquiring knowledge on spiritualism, your ego gets inflated, you think of yourself as superior. The best way is to set aside the subject and forget about it. Then by sheer chance, if you pick up that subject again, it will come from your subconscious through memory and in simple knowing; no ego, go ahead, taste the spirit of action, and experience the fruits.

Although I have explained reality in three different stages, they all form part of the same composite. Is it possible to realize this spiritually enlightened stage of being in super consciousness? Yes! Spiritual sages do attain such enlightenment, but only when they leave behind all attachments and sentiments of materialism, family and friends. Then they become fearless, selfless and compassionate; they live a life of oneness. This may seem impossible to us, but it is important to know, even if it is visionary, what lies on the other end. Even if we cannot reach it, we must attempt to draw closer to that perfection.

We are indeed products of existence in dualities and probably will continue to exist in such a manner. At the same time, on the subject of spiritualism, it is important for us to learn to know all that is needed, about the body, mind and soul. This information provides us with the skills to live a life of purpose and fulfilment. Also, whether it is possible to shine and dance with grace in our existence of dualities, is for you to judge as we continue the journey of understanding begun by sages over 5000 years ago.

That is why, in spirituality, nothingness has a great meaning. It is related to the no-mind zone – a state in which we need to become ego-less to become Self-realized in order to conjoin with the cosmos. We have material realization for the comforts of our body; self-awareness, in which we learn how to liberate ourselves from a life of dualities in realization, which we connect through selfless action in order to be in unison with the one and only spirit. Easterners connect themselves with this nothingness through one of their centring methods, using the art of regulating our breath. Here, the mind disconnects the moment we concentrate on the pattern of breathing/reciting *mantras*/humming *Om* (*aum*), which is a sound, not a word, saluting the vibrations of the cosmic energy prevailing all around.

Today, science and spiritualism are agreed that there is no beginning or end to our universe; we come from nothing and go back into nothing. As explained by the renowned British physicist Stephen Hawking: 'because there is a law such as gravity, the universe can and will create itself from nothing. Spontaneous creation is the reason there is something rather than nothing, why the universe exists, why we exist.' Therefore, empty space is never empty but rather, gives rise to virtual particles and waves, constantly dancing and fluctuating in this nothingness. In fact, the atom, the building block of our universe, comprises of electrons and protons, which has 99.9% empty space, and the rest is still not understood by us.

Nothingness is the ultimate source of knowledge, being the outer perimeter. After that, nothing remains to be known. According to the *Upanishad*s, nothingness is the foundation for something that is understated or of tenuous form. It is the solvent in which anything and everything dissolves. Both scientists and sages agree the universe is infinite; all that is there is energy, indivisible and indestructible, which cannot be created or destroyed. It is said that the planets and stars we are aware of comprise only 4% of what we call the universe; the rest is dark energy, or the unknown.

According to Eastern philosophies, nothingness is designated as a no-mind zone, a state in which one realizes one's own relationship with the cosmos. Stanley Stephen, poet-writer-philosopher, mentions in his book, *The Art of Criticism,* that: 'The Isha Upanishads talk about a very powerful idea – that everything we experience in this world is inhabited and surrounded by *Ishwara* (God).'

Here is an extract from an interesting review of the *Upanishads* by Dennis Littrell, titled 'Important volume on one of humanity's greatest religious works': *In the* Upanishads, *there are two selves. They are symbolized by two birds sitting on a tree branch. The one bird, the self with a small 's' eats. The other bird, the Self with a capital 'S' observes. The first self is the self that is part of this world. The second Self is merely an observer that doesn't take part and is in fact beyond the pairs of opposites such as pleasure and pain that dominate our existence. This Self is formally called the Atman. In an important analogy, it is said that the Atman is the drop of water that glides off of the lotus leaf into the ocean of Brahman, with Brahman being the entirety of all that there is, in other words, God, the God beyond all attribution.*

Littrell reaches the conclusion: *Consciousness is all there is.* The rest, meaning our perceptions, is a personal phenomenon that produces images of limited factors, depending on the individual. Behind all this lies our core energy, as consciousness, illuminating awareness; our link to Brahman, the cosmos, as one, pure, absolute and non-dual. The doctrine further clarifies that *Brahman* (the cosmos), is the only thing that is real and complete – of which we are a part. The material world and its objects are unreal and become decomposed; but soul, in its intelligence, is the spirit, which unites each one of us to the whole.

That is complete, this is complete.
From that completeness comes this completeness;
If we take away this completeness from that
Completeness – only completeness remains…
~ Isha Upanishad

CHAPTER 6
QUANTUM CONSCIOUSNESS

QUANTUM PHYSICS IS A BRANCH of science that deals with indivisible units of energy called quanta. Quantum mechanics, on the other hand, shows the dual behavior of matter, wherein the properties of waves and particles are observed as microscopic objects in atoms. All waves and particles have their own unique frequency, shifting and changing from one position to another; spaceless and timeless. These are the building blocks of everything that exists in the universe, in different vibrations.

---

1. Ernst Schrödinger, *What Is Life?* (1944), 87, http://whatislife.stanford.edu/LoCo_files/What-is-Life.pdf.

For his contribution to wave equation theory in quantum mechanics, Erwin Schrödinger won the Nobel Prize for Physics in 1933. He had a lifelong interest in the Vedanta philosophy of Hinduism, which influenced his thinking that individual consciousness is the manifestation of a unitary consciousness pervading the universe. This theory is now widely accepted by quantum scientists because of the indestructible and indivisible nature of energy.

In *What Is Life?* Schrödinger says: *The earliest records to my knowledge date back some 2,500 years or more. From the early Upanishads, the recognition ATHMAN = BRAHMAN is upheld (the personal self-equals the omnipresent, all-comprehending eternal self). This, in Indian thought, was considered as far from being blasphemous, and represented the quintessence of the deepest insight into the happenings of the world. The striving of all scholars of Vedanta was, after having learnt to pronounce with their lips, to assimilate in their minds this grandest of all thoughts.*[1]

Everything I know about the *Upanishads* and *Advaita* philosophy, regarding non-duality, declares we are one, not two; that *Brahman* (energy), pervades the universe. On observing how identical the theory of quantum physics is to *Brahman*, as explained in the *Upanishad*s, I realized how close science has come to the mysticism of spiritualism. Absoluteness, non-duality and the universe, are one. There is nothing but energy – all pervading, indivisible, indestructible and continuous. Everything is part of that completeness.

Quantum physicists claim this is the ultimate reality, meaning the observer and the observed are the same. In our case, reality becomes limited as the mind observes reality only to the extent of its perceptions, which differs in every individual. Reality, in fact, is timeless; whereas the mind needs time to perceive data through the sense organs and decipher it into thoughts. This is the reason, as already mentioned, that the mind can never be in the now. By the time it perceives now, there is already a new now in place of the old one. Truth, reality, love and the present moment, are a few examples of things the mind can only experience, not perceive.

When in the presence of any moment, the essence of time loses its significance. In the presence of love, time or the mind have little role to play; it is pure experience, which you express in your own way later. In materialism and technology, time is crucial; in spiritual living, timelessness is of vital importance. Timelessness is the no-mind zone – the fountain of creativity, truth, love, awareness and the feeling of oneness. This is what I am attempting to do in this book: unfold the mystery behind experiential living and realization.

Consciousness, in relation to any individual, becomes related to time, space and ego. When consciousness through awareness is directed toward selfless experience, it becomes a part of that network of quantum consciousness that we are all a part of, but separated from. In this manner, even though it is achieved by only a few, when one reaches that ultimate level of total awareness, in which there is no separation between you and me, one becomes eternal by realizing enlightenment, as part of the absolute nature flowing in a spaceless, timeless universe.

On one side of this completeness we have the Absolute and non-dual – our spirit in total awareness of the ultimate reality. On the other, is our existence in duality, again complete in all respects but separated into two, and unfulfilled? Until this energy realizes fulfilment, the spirit or *atman* within keeps wandering in repeated cycles of birth and death until it reaches its origin, when it becomes one again.

How cleverly the cosmos has linked these two in a unified cosmic or quantum consciousness. The human mind keeps borrowing to upgrade its consciousness by manifesting this energy in awareness. The less it borrows the lower is the consciousness. Higher the borrowing, greater is the separation into dual and non-dual, though still remaining in the oneness or completeness of its energy. Regardless of this, the fact is that energy is neither created nor destroyed.

The same cosmic energy, or the Absolute, when it separates, becomes relative; the subject becomes the object, for a short while, in what we refer to as existence. It becomes submerged into duality, in human form; its fulfilment residing deep within.

There is no other reality besides this. Science too, has now conformed to the idea; of one singular continued, universal energy from which all mass or matter springs.

Energy cannot be divided, but it may change its nature from the Absolute by separating into dual or relative. In the same manner, physicists have observed energy superimposed into dual characteristics, appearing simultaneously as wave and particle, sparking and leaping here and there, and not only that, becoming aware, as if they know we are observing them. Similarly, reality gets divided, transferring into duality; existing in separation from its real self as thoughts inundate our minds, classifying everything into this and that.

Through this existence of separation in our minds, desires spring up and we find ourselves wanting everything the mind can perceive. This is why we are happy and unhappy, content and discontented, one being intrinsic to the other, in a search for more and more – all for the self. I believe in this philosophy, but at the same time, I also feel that a super cosmic joke has been played upon us. Only man has the capacity to accept such extremes and become aware of this peculiarity in our existence, swinging like a pendulum, eventually destroying our identity into oneness, unless one has the extreme capacity like the Buddha, to dissolve the body and mind into the eternal spirit.

Though this chapter is a summation of what I have written earlier, a pertinent question crosses the mind, is existence fair, swinging in dualities, conditioned and corrupted in endless desires, accumulations and attachments? Then being also told, that your basic existence itself is nothing but an illusion, living in apparent reality.

It is in our nature to compare, compete, envy and be jealous. No one knows how and why existence functions the way it does. Some call it destiny, past karmas, cause and effect and so on. It may seem unfair, but if existence was to operate by every individual's desires and command, imagine heaven, which no one really knows about, would be a reality on earth for all, and that of course is not possible. What we know is that dualities come in cycles and the apparent unfairness, that we notice is more to balance the continuity of that cycle.

Absolute energy radiates in awareness and dances in oneness, whereas in existence it is separated into me, mine and myself; creating symptoms of anger, despair and anxiety. The subject here is connected to understanding the meaning and significance of oneness. How can we achieve this oneness, which has until now been a mystery and a vision, something for us to just talk about? What happens when we follow and practice selflessness, fearlessness and compassion toward all? How can one bring about a balance between the non-dual and dual, bringing them closer towards the center? I have tried to answer these questions scientifically, spiritually and psychologically, in order to delve deeper into this subject.

Awareness is that pure, pristine, choice-less, changeless, limitless intelligent energy we keep drawing on to raise our consciousness. It originates as intuition or reflexes in the conscious mind, as flashes of creativity. It increases in strength if we are alert and observant. Then comes the subconscious mind, the storehouse of past awareness and thoughts, in the form of memory.

We have to become aware of past awareness, which may have been channeled into negativity by thoughts, especially for those involved in nefarious activities. There are also instances of the mind, while sleeping or dreaming, experiencing awareness in a sublime or disengaged state. Hence, we sometimes awaken to find the answer which has been eluding us.

We understand that gross and subtle energy, in the form of body and mind, decomposes on death and returns to earth. What happens then, to all the intelligent energy stored within us as self-knowledge, awareness and realization, in the form of core thoughts, soul or *atman*? Whether it transmigrates into a new cycle of birth and death, as claimed by the *Upanishad*s in Vedanta, has yet to be proven.

But many scriptures claim that the energy of life is eternal and continues as absolute in its nature. Existence in duality revolves in its cycle of birth and death; with such energy remaining in the periphery, separated from its center until it becomes one. As body and mind are limited and decompose, life continues, while the self or soul keeps wandering into innumerable cycles of birth and death. We only reach that final stage of existence when we realize total awareness in pure consciousness, becoming Absolute. Then the soul dissolves into the network of quantum consciousness, to become eternal.

Such a soul is distinguished as God at this final stage of completeness in pure consciousness. The meaning of God has been defined, scripted and translated as existence in total awareness and is pure bliss.

Even though knowledge of the Self as pure consciousness, and enlightenment by realizing God in total awareness, to become the Absolute, may be the ultimate purpose of life, it is important to know what lies at both ends - from ego to pure consciousness. We live in both material and spiritual reality. Only then, can one experience and understand the difference, making awareness and enlightenment possible.

We should not suppress the ego, desire, Satan, or lust within. By being suppressed, they remain. Just witness and watch, without forming an attitude for or against through non-attachment, and become aware. Gradually, we begin to rise towards the center of these extremes, with our eyes open.

You are what your deepest desire is;
As is your desire, so is your intention;
As is your intention, so is your will;
As is your will, so is your deed;
As is your deed, so is your destiny…
~ Upanishads

CHAPTER 7
AWAKENING

SPIRITUALITY IS NOT MERELY SEEKING, searching or desiring. It can only be realized in living through its practices. It is an ongoing process; it starts from the day of realization that there is some energy within and around us that is beyond mind, time and thought. Thoughts, though supreme, are generally used for the external or material world, leading to both comfort and suffering. In spiritualism, this is referred to as being in body consciousness.

We are told repeatedly that we need to go deep within to realize the real nature of our inner self.

This going inward is a metaphor; the answer lies not in going deeper but in our basic, simple understanding of life. It tells us that whatever we may possess or accumulate (perhaps a house on the beach or in the mountains, love for our family and friends, wealthy, frequent holidays), there will definitely be something missing, a gap of loneliness and despair. Spiritual awakening is necessary to fill the void.

We exist and function via our thoughts. Whether it is knowledge, emotion, awareness, or consciousness, deep down it is thoughts that interpret the significance of each. Thoughts are dependent on how fast we collect data from the five senses. After that, the mind, through its power of thought, discriminates and chooses, for its own interests, pursuing its desires. To balance and control, the mind has the power of reason to limit desires and draw extra energy in the form of awareness, to witness its activities – all in relation to thought.

On the other hand, in spiritualism, time and speed have no relevance. Here, action, experience and realization play key roles in witnessing our thoughts, through awareness.

By witnessing our own thoughts, we awaken that pure intelligent energy to manifest the awareness in our minds. There is an awakening within oneself; we begin to realize that there is another us, bigger than our identified *I*, hidden within our physical self, our consciousness. Science, although accustomed to physical mass or matter in all shapes, forms and sizes, is still baffled by this invisible consciousness.

When energy interacts with the mind, it manifests as awareness, and becomes the subject of any situation. Remember that one is the subject, the aware being, including the body and mind in relation to 'who' one is. The content of our aware being, in turn, becomes the essence of your consciousness as 'what' you are. Since our minds can exist only in dualities, this energy gets separated into two, so awareness then penetrates in any direction, positive or negative, depending on space, time and the circumstance influencing it at that moment.

Metaphysics calls this consciousness soul, spirit or *atman*. If awareness, which is responsible for making the mind aware to be conscious, is not there, we will be completely lost in the restless chattering of our minds. Awareness navigates our thinking through the degree of individual consciousness, in a direct link to cosmic energy. The higher the degree of consciousness, greater is our awakening in self-realization. In simple terms, this means that thoughts lead us toward self-desires unless spiritualism comes to make us aware and balance this insanity. This alignment between spirit, mind and body is what spiritualism is all about. Spiritualism is the study that takes us beyond our normal thinking capacity to a level of awareness at which we realize who and what we really are.

In the case of animals, awareness is limited to the present moment, to distinguishing between this and that, through short-term memory. A human being, however, awakened to the power of awareness, is able to develop his consciousness and connect to his past, present and future. He can discriminate and choose thoughts and emotions using his intellect, and combine awareness and consciousness to reveal his intent in order to experience any situation.

It is said that life gives us what is destined for us; our thoughts and deeds are restricted only to those results that are in our destiny. In my understanding, life gives us what we intend to take from it, and that is what we receive. Existence revolves around our intentions to the extent that we really wish strongly for something; cosmic intelligence and creative, intuitive awareness join forces with our intellect and emotions, to achieve results that may, in fact, be far beyond our capacity to imagine.

Life or cosmic energy will always respond to our intentions, especially if we are totally convinced in body, mind and soul, because in reality we are what our deepest desire yearns for. Thus, destiny and *karma* are two sides of the same coin; they need to coexist in any situation to determine results. We may give the past, as a credit to destiny, but our today is in our hands. It is today which is going to make your destiny for tomorrow. It is today, which you decide through your intentions, where destiny can play no role.

There are also moments when our awareness may drag us into a negative zone. If our mind is obsessed with negativity and has blocked positive channels, we start desiring negativity, and that is what we receive. What then, is the answer?

For instance, we may notice or realize that we are driven toward fear or greed. Despite knowing their harmful effects, we remain entrapped. We then need to become further aware to decide how to get out. This dilemma gives us the chance to go deeper into the same field or escape, depending on how we handle the situation and existing circumstances. This is where your personal power or your individuality comes in.

Note that this has no connection to enlightenment. We are only at the stage of awareness now. Our deeds have yet to follow, to affect the outcome. Spiritual celebrities, who are highly aware, speak about discarding the ego, being in the now, and say, that wealth is behind all evil. However, we can see in their deeds that they are imprisoned in ego-consciousness, desiring more and more wealth and fame, either for themselves or for their institutions. It is rare to come across people like Gandhi and Mandela, who have become eternal through their actions and sacrifices. Their names and faces were never flashed in the media with the intention of personal gain, but because of their selfless sacrifices and love for the people, they cherished.

If there is desire, fear, and greed on one hand, taking us toward material realization, there is also selflessness, fearlessness and compassion, leading us towards divinity, on the other. This tug-of-war between self-progress and mental peace, will always exist, with the former taking center stage up to the age of 40 or so; from 40-60, we exist between the two. The remaining years are probably dedicated to the latter. In my opinion, this is the right approach. Only after material progress can one truly understand self-actualization. There is always awareness hidden in our individuality, to guide us to our limits in any field of progress.

Ego is inherent and intrinsic. It is a part of who we are; our mind is nothing but ego. Only others can observe our degree of ego; we may realize it, but it remains with us. It should neither be suppressed nor negated. It is we in our identity, and our shadow, which we need to understand and respect since we cannot do without it. Life is a paradox; the same ego that is so necessary for external representation becomes detrimental to our inner peace and tranquility, making it negative.

In success, negative ego can become the cause of

failure if we allow it to rule us. Yet it should never be suppressed; we need to accept and surrender to this ego in humility, and experience the flow of love that comes in return. Only then, can we rationalize and become aware of both the positive and negative effects of ego. This awareness, in turn, helps us accept ego with grace. We can then let go of what is unfavorable in a natural manner, going with the flow of life.

Likewise, if we wish to awaken spiritually, we are required to be alert and observant, understand and accept, be aware of any situation in totality, our likes and dislikes, progress, knowledge and the depth of our existence in duality. We are gifted, among all other creatures, to have been born as human, with the power to discriminate, choose and enjoy the dichotomies of life. If we do not accept the paradoxes (explained in detail later), they suck us into ignorance. If fulfilment in life is our purpose, we do need to understand the concept of the Absolute, non-dual, and pure consciousness: everything is one, not two. Life itself is a paradox, in order to experience, the only way is to know the opposites. You will not understand truth, God, health or happiness until you have experienced its opposite. Awareness emerges in the mind, only to comprehend and understand the dualities or opposites. Therefore, just be, surrender and accept both in grace, and flow in harmony.

Nothing is total or complete in our minds if we are not aware of the other extreme of any duality. I am not implying that you follow a life of non-duality; fulfilment demands that existence should be experienced in totality. This comes when we understand and experience both ends, in balance – when both extremes meet in their center to become one and absolute. Existential living is experiential realization: we need to live it rather than just know about it.

In order to awaken, flow simply in life, but with a deeper understanding of our energies: gross, which is in the body, for health; subtle, which is in the mind, through thoughts; and core, which comes from the spirit. Next comes spatial energy, which exists in space; you can draw on it through awareness. These will make you aware of different layers of living: superficial (external), peripheral (Separated from our inner core), internal (to align body mind and spirit as one). It is unnecessary to prove to anyone that we are somebody.

Existence does not mean living like a child, in innocence and ignorance. Life is complex and confusing. We want to simplify our lives as much as possible, knowing, understanding, and experiencing both ends of duality. Accept things on equal terms, moving toward their center or totality in oneness with the universe from which they have been separated. Good or bad, God or Devil, positive or negative, all add up to the same completeness, in the totality of life. Only then are we able to self-realize that if the ego is essential, so are compassion and empathy. If wealth and comforts are important, so is our duty to oneness, for our fulfilment, completeness with self and spirit or *atman*.

To recapitulate, the mind revolves around our emotions and desires. Our intellect gives us the power to reason, discriminate and choose. Our awareness makes us conscious of our thoughts, deeds and actions. Becoming aware of our awareness leads us forward on the journey we decide based on our unique individuality, what relationship we wish to have between our inner and external being.

Alignment of the physical, mental,
social and spiritual, is the art of living.

CHAPTER 8
ART OF LIVING

THE SUBTLE ART OF LIVING lies in the fulfilment of our physical, mental, financial, social and spiritual needs. It is only through good health, both mental and physical, that we can accumulate wealth, give back something to society, and become spiritually wise. It is the alignment of these in the order given that brings fulfilment and completeness in totality.

Spiritual living appears at the end of this list for it is only through spiritual realization that we go beyond thought. This happens when we are content.With our physical needs taken care of, we are ready to attain a higher consciousness in spiritual reality. Going beyond perceptive thoughts then becomes necessary. As long as the mind is involved, thoughts of desire are bound to be present. With the perceptual mind, we can achieve money, fame and power, but for peace and joy, we require the help of spiritualism. That is why in the Western world, where there is an abundance of wealth, one is what one thinks, but in the East, more influenced by spiritualism, one is when one does not think.

Thoughts have a tendency, through narrow-mindedness, to function only for self-interest and self-desire, to keep seeking this or that through discrimination and choice. When we go beyond such thoughts, we reach a stage of mindfulness, of living in the present, from one moment to the next: alert, observant and aware; understanding, accepting and surrendering our ego, not to any person but to our own self. That is when, in order to transform and grow, we are able to experience the present, what we are doing and experiencing, rather than analyzing its merits and demerits. To go beyond the mind into the intuitive world, we must be alert, observant and aware, like animals are. We must understand and then accept, indulge in, and outgrow, what we do not approve of, in order to transform into a higher consciousness.

The art of living is not in renouncing or suppressing what we do not like, but rather in accepting everything with total respect. It raises us in life so we become more knowing than questioning. We indulge in experiences rather than compare and analyze them; thus we reduce the discriminatory and egoistical mind in favor of experiential living, using appropriate methods to adjust our ego-consciousness to achieve peace and balance. This way we have fewer conflicts, more experience, and wisdom in any act. What we do not like drops effortlessly from our awareness, disappearing on its own, without our mind telling us to give it up.

Suppose you have, a stone in your pocket that you think is a diamond. A jeweler tells you it is just glass, and shows you the way to verify this. Naturally, now that you have become aware, the stone drops from your hand automatically, and you simply ignore it; there is no conflict.

When we understand and recognize negative behavior, we outgrow it and become wiser, without any mental resistance. The next time we will not easily mistake a stone for a diamond. All creatures behave in this manner, except us. We bring in our calculating mind, totally in self-interest, using its power to discriminate and choose – which may be a blessing but is also a curse, for while there are the benefits of choice, it also leads to conflicts and anxiety.

Home is the center at which we all meet and reside. Similarly, our core energy, our spirit, our being in awareness, balances and controls our thoughts, which are constantly chattering and demanding more and more. We need to realize how important it is to unite the three energies into one. This is our center, our true home. Why is it essential that we remain in the right rhythm and vibration? Because the distortion is the cause of physical and mental ailments.

Both gross (body) and subtle energy (mind) are generally detached from our core, creating confusion by and leading us into a paradoxical life. Thus, we may have everything and still have nothing. This occurs when our thoughts are supreme, creating a separation by thinking only of ourselves. This separation of our thoughts from totality is the cause of our restlessness and disturbance. We feel there is something missing in life, and end up reading books on self-development. Uniting these three energies should be the basic purpose in life; otherwise, we are bound to remain in sorrow and suffering.

Most spiritual gurus negate the 'I' or ego, since it thrives only in body consciousness. Overruling the 'I' is not easy. Our realization of peace and tranquility comes only after having attained all we can from this material world. Moreover, how will we become awakened, liberated or enlightened in the absence of 'I'? Prior to the formation of ego, there was no need to know anything else; we were simple. It is because of this identification with ego that we have become what we are. This being the reason, detachment towards, ego, desire and sentimentalism are more significant than non-attachment. It is only when you know how to lie, that the relevance of truth emerges.

Whatever anyone might tell us, our basic reality remains our ego, desires, identity and perceptions. It is not that we do not agree with them; but life is such a paradox that anyone's reality is only what they can observe with their perceptions. Each one's reality remains their individuality, through their personal power. This reality keeps changing according to time, space, circumstance, knowledge, awareness and experiences. The *Upanishads* declare that, through righteous means, we must first acquire wealth and fulfil all desires, so we are free to understand what liberation and spiritual freedom is all about.

The degree of spiritual growth is directly proportionate to personal freedom. The person, who is dependent on social and religious beliefs or blindly agrees with and follows what others say without using his own power of reasoning, clearly shows a lack of spiritual and inner freedom. By mechanically following others, he can never reach far, for he loses his individuality and uniqueness.

For this very reason, Buddha declared: *"Believe nothing, no matter where you read it, or who said it, no matter if I have said it, unless it agrees with your own reason and your own common sense"* – Buddha

The answer to this riddle of existence lies in balancing the apparent reality of what we are with the constant cosmic reality. First, we need to obtain knowledge of Self and learn how to be true to it. Self-awareness comes next – awakening to the ignorance about the life we exist in. To understand, know and indulge in experiential realization, is to be able to accept life in totality. This aligns our external identity with our consciousness, enabling us to obtain the experience of accepting both happiness and sadness with equal grace.

We also need to remember that knowledge or intelligent energy can flow in either direction, positive or negative. That is why I emphasize on being aware of our own awareness, particularly past awareness, which turns into thoughts and settles into our subconscious, the memory bank. The real nature of awareness is never fully defined. Unless we are true to our own selves, any spiritual exercise we undertake is futile. It seems silly to write '*Be true to your own self*'; but so often we are not. There is always something up our sleeve, providing excuses, so our mind can think we are always right. That is what the ego is all about. Whatever our inner beliefs, our subconscious creates the conditions to support them. The conscious and subconscious are needed to act in unison, in order to create that transformation within.

The only way out of such dualities is to accept both with grace. Opposites are nothing but two ends of the same whole. At their center, the energy is one; only our emotions are separate. Even though essentially one, the mind is helpless; it cannot accept both together, because of its power to discriminate and choose. It can be done only when we bypass the mind and accept both dualities without conditions, thus gaining access to our true nature in totality.

Science too says, that only opposites can meet, because the same repels the other. You will notice that only the positive and negative meet, with the neutral or the earth, balancing the two. The mind will keep separating in self-interest; it will apply logic more towards your favor. Only love and truth can neutralize what the mind may consider as positive or negative.

What I am saying may seem absurd or strange by logic, mind or many intellectuals. My contention here is ego and desire in self-interest, from body and mind, are all that external perceptual thoughts are made of. You just cannot over-rule or ridicule for long, unless you renounce, suppress or control, which really is not the solution.

Be alert and aware, of whatever the mind does, this witnessing, observing, surrendering and accepting both opposites in grace is what I am asking. Just be as you are in watchfulness and notice the difference, the same shall bring forth in the flow of your life.

Mind, which is consumed and alert in its own silent flow is higher than that of a spiritual mind trying to fool itself by claiming it has no ego.

If you consider both with equal respect, the ugliness or the obsession of both start to disappear and you balance and live more with your presence in awareness rather than just perceptual thoughts. You will experience and realize that it is the wholeness of anything and everything, which provides the complete meaning. Only chanting mantras like the monks do, is not going to get you anywhere in life. You are here to enjoy and celebrate, with a full mind, but in alertness and awareness. So be it, do not negate the evil or the devil, they are also a part of you.

Awareness can emerge only from its opposites, in order to make your consciousness aware and rise. Each moment is sacred, whether good or bad. It depends on the way you look at it. If your attitude is negative, your journey will be of anguish and anxiety. However, if you look at any situation in every moment, with acceptance and awareness, sacredness is bound to flourish within you.

Body, mind and spirit are like the points of a triangle; we need to bring them to their center. This center is most important, as it brings the required balance, which we then radiate in life. This centring relaxes our energies and stills the mind to the level of tranquility we desire. This center is our purpose – where mind, body and spirit interact with love and acceptance.

My journey started with the presumption that I was going to achieve wonders through spiritualism. The devious, devilish, materialistic nature in me did not wish to give up anything. However, after gaining some spiritual knowledge, I realized there was nothing to renounce or attain. For, if on one side we have duality, then on the other, is non-duality. This also is a paradox. Even if I became highly positive, my negative side would always be there, intrinsically linked, waiting to embrace me the moment I succumbed to any unfavorable situation or circumstance.

Therefore, I learned that the only answer to this sort of experiential living lies in the mind; in accepting both parts of duality as one, with grace and respect; by accepting both the positive and the negative in the righteous or moral manner. When we experience both in spiritual freedom, we notice the dualities starting to move toward their center in oneness.

Both will gradually stop affecting and bothering us if we handle each with equal respect, not allowing the mind to tell us how to analyze, discriminate and choose between them. In reality, selecting anything, whether positive or negative, is simple; leave it to awareness, to spontaneity. It is just the mind, which makes things complicated. For instance, take God and the Devil as one. If we suppose there is no Devil, there will be no need for God either.

Gurus often tell us that our actions should be like a child's – without complexities and ego; simple, divine and full of godliness. However, we forget that a child is ignorant, and that is not the case with us. We need to understand that besides accumulating knowledge and living a life of materialism, comfort and technology, we also need to learn the art of accepting and loving unconditionally, with grace and awareness in practice.

In our existence within this world of space and time, absolute pure energy enters with oneness, as unconditional love. Love is the only energy that fulfills giving as well as receiving. Love is the essence of our being. However, in order to exist, we function through the mind, which fragments and divides even love into its duality of choice. Love then changes to conditions of expectations and preferences, according to time and space, and can turn to hate and back again to love.

The art of living is incomplete if it is not accompanied by the awakening of our spiritual self – existentially and experientially. This becomes possible only for those who possess a strong sense of their own, individual common sense and personal power, devotion and love for the welfare of all in the universe.

Liberation, in spiritual terms, means understanding how to release oneself from the ignorance of existence in duality or apparent reality. For this, we need to awaken in spiritual knowledge, awareness and experience, and so reach the pivot on which we can balance ourselves. Materialism may be most important to mind and body by the laws of economics, but the real art of living is to first realize the right balance and center between any two dual forces within our own individuality; and how far we wish to go in bringing them together.

Practicing experiential living in total acceptance and respect, with physical, mental, social and spiritual understanding, is to live in harmony.

You may exist as body and mind,
but in absolute you dissolve;
In existence there is sorrow; in absolute there is bliss;
In existence there is change; in absolute there is reality;
In existence you are known; in absolute you are energy;
In existence you are thought; in absolute total awareness;
In existence you are matter; in absolute you are spirit.

CHAPTER 9
REALITY & EXISTENCE

WHO DECIDES WHAT REALITY IS? We do. What we observe and experience becomes our reality, and what is invisible becomes mystical. *Brahman*, the all-pervasive spirit, was as of recently, invisible, mystical, the way non-duality is today. However, when science penetrated deep into the subatomic level of matter with high-powered microscopes, it observed nothing but indivisible energy, discreetly exhibiting its properties, timeless and space-less. Physicists then concluded what the Upanishads said millennia ago – that everything exists as energy, in absolute reality.

Reality is absolute; it contains all that exists. Existence is more of a subset of reality. That which is unreal cannot exist, but there may be certain factors, which are real but do not exist, like a mathematical number. In general terms, existence is more related to objects to be real. But then again if anything in existence keeps changing, it is referred to as apparent reality.

Like you may say, our mind and body keeps changing, originating from dust and going back into dust. Such an apparent reality is still deemed real, because the content of the absolute, remains constant and interchangeable in both forms of matter or energy. This is because both science and spiritualism consider energy interchangeable, from one into another, with the basic real constituent remaining the same.

When we say our existence is more of an illusion, it is considered more in the way we look at our existence, which keeps changing, than its factuality. Therefore, reality is required more in its absoluteness of its content, to be referred to as the ultimate reality.

Reality needs to be observed and perceived to come to any firm conclusion. Now comes the difficult part: consciousness which is the faculty of perception through our series of experiences via thoughts and awareness, does that exist or not?

In order to exist, we have given this name as energy, irrespective of its form. It has to actually exist, rather than imagined or appearing to exist. So in a wider definition, we are compelled to conclude that reality, whether comprehensible or not, does exist objectively, experientially and in the absolute. All are synonymous to each other, to the extent being that reality and existence are the same. To distinguish between the three becomes difficult. In the most simplistic terms, let us define reality as that which actually exists.

Similarly, we should not discard non-duality. For, non-duality is nothing but the absolute. It is agreed that it is not achievable in the normal course of living, but knowledge of non-duality becomes imperative in order to know the totality of existence. Non-duality, in fact, is nothing but absoluteness in the form of pure energy. However, when it manifests in the mind as thoughts, fragments and separates into duality, so we can choose between opposites. This choice formulates our character and intentions.

In duality, we have the luxuries of technology and materialism, leading us to comforts and separating us from the purity of our true nature. Here the mind progresses with ego on its side. At the other extreme is pure non-duality, absolute energy, providing experiential enlightenment toward oneness. So what are we supposed to do?

The nearer we come to the center of the two extremes of any duality, the more in balance is our existence. The more we move towards non-duality, the better and closer we are to oneness or quantum consciousness. Since we are all tilted toward duality, is it not relevant to learn and indulge its opposite, non-duality, to achieve the required balance? The degree of our consciousness determines which side we are more prone to and defines our reality and existence.

This way, the mind-body relationship, in existence with dualities, continues its cycle of birth and death.

The body comes from energy and goes back to it, but life sustains intelligent energy into a new existence in one continuum; it just exists. Therefore, when we look at the world through our perceptions, it is illusionary, apparent, and limited; constantly changing through cause and effect.

With higher awareness, we become conscious. The mind becomes more subjective than objective, illusions start to drop away and we realize how narrow the mind is. This is the reason for all our despair and grief. We enter into higher levels of consciousness; our individuality starts to dissolve into its basic and fundamentally, unchangeable reality, like sugar or salt loses its own identity in water.

This dissolution of consciousness into the oneness of the universe is called quantum consciousness and this web of unitary consciousness is our fundamental reality and purpose in life. It comes with unconditional love, devotion and selflessness, and is not restricted to space, time or individual matter. It is related to cosmic consciousness and connects each of us in a web of past, present and future, as one whole.

We need such an awakening to liberate ourselves from the constant bickering of our lonely separated selves, to enlighten ourselves not in words and preaching but in our deeds of compassion and appreciation for everything that surrounds us. This is the true meaning of life. Otherwise, as is so apparent today, despite having everything in abundance, we remain unhappy and discontented.

In quantum reality, waves and particles within energy show bizarre and paradoxical dual properties. On observation, it behaves strangely, as both a particle and a wave, simultaneously leaping and sparking in multiple places, defying space and time. However, it is also aware of being observed. In the same manner, our own consciousness also has dual or quantum-like properties, as both functions are within their own substratum of energy.

When we observe our consciousness, we notice properties parallel to quantum energy. Even though perception is all we have, when we observe ourselves, we notice that our thoughts are never still, but jumping from one to another, never consistently in any one place. In a matter of seconds, we can travel to any corner of the world and back, in the mind. We are unable to focus our thoughts and self-consciousness in one fixed place or time for long. Thoughts are similar to virtual particles in quantum mechanics. This is why most spiritual gurus teach us how to meditate and focus, telling us how and why to be in the present, from one moment to another. Presence has awareness, and in awareness, there is presence.

The centring of our consciousness through awareness or quantum borrowing, requires a certain order, which takes us to an inner state, awakening us to a reality where, if we wish for harmony and balance, we need to live with singular consciousness, in surrender and acceptance.

Scientists have observed the same: whatever dual properties our individual consciousness might have, eventually only one reality remains supreme. It is a simple case of an observer being separate from what is being observed, though both are nothing but energy. To put this in high-flown words, our universe is a hermetic, holographic whole in which we will come and go, but in which life flows eternally.

To recapitulate, absoluteness or non-duality becomes the subject and our world in duality is the object – each projecting itself as a singular whole.

Similarly, quantum mechanics explains that all is energy, even if its nature is to separate and exhibit duality. Yet it remains and survives as an indestructible whole.

Many disagree with this spiritual philosophy of non-duality, absoluteness or oneness, as they consider subject and object distinct and separate from one another. From that subject, however, comes any object, both complete, dissolving back into the other. This has been beautifully interpreted and translated from the *Upanishad*s. Although I mentioned this passage earlier, I would like to repeat it here:

That is complete, this is complete. From that completeness comes this completeness; if we take away this completeness from that completeness, only completeness remains.

We live within a world of paradoxes, where things are seldom what they seem. This applies to most aspects of our lives, since our existence is dependent on dualities or opposites. In order to define or understand anything, we have to rely on its position in a dichotomy, and relate it to something we find meaningful. So what is real or good for one may be unreal and bad for the other. For example, life would have no meaning without us knowing about death. This is where paradoxes come in, confusing us and making our lives imbalanced and inadequate. Therefore, reality as it pertains to our existence is uncertain, as it changes with time and space.

It is only after experience in *karma* (action), that we may understand the fulfilment of knowledge. *Karma yoga* spiritually demands selfless action, with no personal reward. At the other extreme, we have mind-body, designed to demand and want more and more from life. Both are necessary: one for material wealth and the other for spiritual wealth. Here, centring is required, in which we must accept and act in totality, rather than allow the mind to think otherwise. We cannot disregard any extreme;

both are a part of the same completeness. We have to accept both without tilting toward one, whether positive-negative, good/bad or God/Devil. We must remain as close to the center as we can.

The more we understand that physical reality as given by our perceptions is uncertain, due to constant changes, the more confusing it becomes. Science has also clarified that images that appear in the mind are quite different from factual reality. Further confusion is created by the fact that substantial characteristics of our experiences do not exhibit themselves in actual reality when observed scientifically. For example, each of us experiences a particular color in a shade distinct from what any other person sees; the vibration of sound, for that matter, is also a different experience for each listener. This has confused science for a long time. Even now, science has not been able to understand the mystery behind subjective experiences that form our consciousness through awareness.

Spiritualism has always maintained that all objective reality is an illusion; what is real is consciousness

– which remains eternally transmigrating as soul, from one cycle of birth and death to another. The interesting factor to note here is that consciousness, as a subjective experience, explained above, is expressed uniquely in each of us. Therefore, for consciousness to exist in any mind, it can only be self-consciousness. For this reason, I have emphasized personal power, individuality and uniqueness throughout this book. We remain distinct identities in the form of self-consciousness.

Since we cannot exist in exclusion of one another, so consciousness too, cannot exist without being within the grid of oneness, in continuum as cosmic consciousness. This is how impersonal intelligence-energy, through awareness manifesting in mind, becomes personal in the form of self-consciousness. It then participates in all the deeds and subjective experiences of existence, so that it may continue its journey into the next existence – until it reaches the goal of becoming pure and liberated energy.

This phenomenon of intelligence-energy, converting itself from impersonal to personal, and then reaching forward to pure consciousness or back into its total awareness, and then realizing enlightenment, may seem bizarre, mysterious and mystical. However, enlightened souls like Buddha, Jesus and Krishna, who achieved liberation from the dualities of existence in absolute self-surrender, and attained pure consciousness, have lived in the fellowship spiritualism refers to as single unified consciousness. Like beads on a thread, each one has their own identity, but all are strung together into one necklace.

Therefore, reality remains permanent and changeless, not being affected by time and space; it can neither be created nor destroyed. However, the shades of reality differ; each in its own uniqueness remains distinct, while finally joining in one continuum to form the completeness of the whole.

From this evolves the meaning of God: *To exist in pure consciousness is bliss.* Though the enlightened soul in pure consciousness attains the status of God, it never loses its individuality while existing eternally in that unified consciousness.

Duality is to exist; non-duality is divine.

CHAPTER 10
NON-DUALITY

EDUCATION, SCIENCE AND SPIRITUALISM, teach us not to be carried away by dogmas or blind beliefs. We are also told that realities are those facts of existence that can be observed, measured and experienced. Only then are we convinced that what we believe is true. Can the same logic be applied to our belief in God? Billions of people all over the world have faith in God without knowing whether He exists or not. Faith or fear, drive them forward. Different religions often divide people by making them believe there are different gods for different groups. In my opinion, it is an individual's right to determine and understand the concept of God.

The Eastern world, for thousands of years, has proclaimed that everything that exists is nothing but indestructible, non-dual energy, in the form of one spirit – God. In their scriptures on non-duality and the essence of Advaita, the *Upanishads* say that supreme knowledge is bestowed on him who understands and realizes *tat tvam asi* (thou art that), *tat* (the ultimate reality), *tvam* (*brahman*/spirit/energy), and *asi* (self). This simply means: 'I am That' – the formless, infinite and all-pervasive self.

Thinking of oneself as an individual separate from God is an illusion, because we are not two, but one, pervading this universe in a single source called *brahmn*, which is indivisible and which cannot be created nor destroyed. To realize this state is to become divine or enlightened. Until then, we remain separate, in duality, existing in ignorance, loneliness and pain. How mystical, but true.

What the sages said thousands of years ago is being found to be true in labs today, after years of research costing billions of dollars. Science has discovered we are all energy, which is absolute, though it changes form or structure. What we perceive to be real or true is nothing but an optical illusion.

The *Upanishads* declare: *When we divide anything by nothing (energy) we get infinity, and when we divide anything by infinity, we get nothing.* This is how the integer zero was introduced to the world. Both energy and zero are similar; they emerge from nothing, remain on their own until they merge, and manifest. In our study, energy reveals its presence by joining with matter to become body and mind; the other manifests by quantifying numerically.

Many Westerners come to India in pursuit of spiritual enlightenment, but return dejected. This is due to their expectation of attaining liberation, enlightenment, or some magical turnaround of their sorrows. They discover there is nothing to seek or obtain except dropping their illusions. They go back disappointed, for there is nothing that can be given or received. The point is to awaken from our existence of ignorance, in which we exist in separation, and realize that we are one.

There is nothing to gain from whatever anyone preaches or the books we may read. Energy remains the same; God and we remain one absolute reality in total awareness, consciousness, spirit, or whatever else we may want to call it. Non-duality and duality are just reference points in our existence; we exist somewhere in the gap between the two, separated from the center.

As we have learned, God is at one end but the Devil is on the other – they conjoin in the center. They are two sides of the same coin, separated from each other; for without the Devil, the need for God would not exist. It is how, where, and in what manner we accept the dualities existing in the mind, and how we experience, realize and flow with them, that is the subject of this book. Most of us, when dejected with life, wonder why, even after achieving so much with our efforts, we are still disturbed and restless. Then how do we handle this volatile mind – chattering endlessly and creating anxieties and despair?

We are undoubtedly in the rat race, which pushes us to want more and more. By allowing our minds to reach a high degree of self-centeredness, we are unable to find sanity, instead creating anxiety, fear and despair. This is when awareness dawns, and we ask ourselves, now what? Do we continue in this rat race or retreat? We need to know what else there is in life besides searching for wealth, technology, comfort and luxury, in order to improve our quality of life.

First, what we must understand is that spirituality is not attained by pursuit. It is possible only by living it. Enlightenment is a pure and personal experience. Spiritual living is going with the flow: knowing, accepting and doing our *karma*s in totality, and being more proactive than reactive. The mind is limited by its thoughts of choosing/deciding, until it reaches the stage when it understands all things using knowledge and experience. Then, the *karma*s take over and the concept of 'me and mine' becomes far less important. Even when there is material dissatisfaction, there will definitely be overall contentment from total acceptance in every situation.

We live in a world of paradoxes, where things are seldom what they seem. Existence is in duality, and paradox is inherent in it. Even though the dictionary defines 'paradox' as something self-contradictory and even absurd, in dual reality, it has an element of truth. We are told that opposites cannot exist together: it is either this or that, but not both. The mind refuses to accept that in happiness, tears can fall, but it does happen.

This is where paradoxes come in, confusing us and making us feel off-balance and inadequate. Today, we buy more but enjoy less, we have bigger houses but smaller families, more knowledge but less wisdom, more medicines but less wellness. We have technology to save time but still we are always short of time. We fall in love, but do not know the meaning of how to rise in love.

The mind is designed to separate and focus on only one portion of the whole. It lacks totality, keeping us isolated and disjointed. This is the reason we have more of everything but enjoy it less – more knowledge but less common sense, and so much wealth but more poverty. The irony is highlighted so well in these few lines from one of my favorite prayers by St. Francis of Assisi: *For it is in giving that we receive; it is in pardoning that we are pardoned; and it is in dying that we are born to eternal life.*

Paradoxes in life defy their apparent meanings as they all eventually meet deep within as one. We can never be complete without comprehending opposites as being one. For example, there are two banks of a river, each with different surroundings, yet both form a part of the same body of water.

Contradictions originate from the mind and its limited perceptions. The earth revolves around the sun; one part, facing it, has day, and the other night; though in reality, at the center, both are one. Similarly, genders may separate into male and female at birth, though they originated as one at fertilization. Genders are interconnected throughout existence, clinging to each other, and each having some hormonal characteristics of the other.

In the cycle of birth and death, genders may remain separate, as extremes, but eventually the body decomposes and the soul transmigrates back into energy or spirit, as one, regardless of gender. In the same way, sadness is intrinsic to happiness; if one is present, there is bound to be its separated other half lurking near. Laughter and tears, sound and silence, truth and lies, all are nothing but two ends of the same oneness. Each part cannot exist without the other. If we identify and cling to either end, we suffer. However, if we transcend by not allowing the mind to separate them, we will have better acceptance and control over any situation, positive or negative.

In spiritual living, before the mind can discriminate and choose between this and that in a narrow, selfish approach, we should accept all that there is in totality, both positive and negative, and dissolve into any situation. That way, like animals who respond to stimuli instinctively for self-preservation, we are bound to reject what is not suitable and so function in totality, accepting whatever comes with respect and able to transform without bias.

Most importantly, in this theory of acceptance in totality, we allow opposites to draw closer towards the center. Make the mind a witness to both. While it cannot change any circumstance, it can observe, definitely without becoming a victim through its choices. Remember, choices lead to conflict. If both are accepted with equal grace, there cannot be conflict. Accept them both. In this way, we refrain from and leave behind what we do not like.

Detach the mind and body from duality, from our identifications and attachments in any situation, and become one. We then become the master of our mind, transcending its normal functioning rather than living in a cycle of madness, misery and despair. In this manner, spiritualism explains that everything that pervades this universe is not two but one. No one thing can exist in exclusion of the other.

Then there are no prejudices, preferences, negations, comparisons or judgments from the mind. This benefits the self, as actions are performed in awareness, without allowing the mind to separate; thus, there is oneness and purity. Non-duality is just that: nothing but pure, absolute spirit or energy. We may read or write books on spirituality, but unless we experience and realize the same existentially, there is no enlightenment, and the pursuit is futile. Jesus, Buddha and a few others, realized enlightenment in this way – through self-sacrifice and by accepting it all with grace, in unified consciousness.

Psychology differs from spiritualism here. Psychology goes deep into explaining the logic and effects of each dichotomy with plurality and objectivity; it is concerned more with the interaction of the mind with the outer world; about existence. Psychology speaks of thoughts, sensations and perceptions. Spiritualism, on the other hand, being singular and subjective, is the study of the inner realm within us. It refutes dichotomy. It says everything is one: the sum total of our experiences forming a unit called life. Spiritualism refers to this as the real 'I', which experiences all that the mind does. It reminds us that scientific knowledge is based on the perception and observation of objects. But human intelligence is eventually based on personal experiences through the consciousness of life in its totality.

When you believe in God you exist;
When you understand God you transcend;
When you accept God you transform;
When you realize God you are one.

CHAPTER 11
THREE STAGES OF EXISTENCE
IN EASTERN THOUGHT

EASTERN SCRIPTURES DELVE DEEPLY into spirituality and human existence bound by duality and paradoxes. As we have seen, they divide spirituality into three stages. The first is self-knowledge or *Brahman* (spirit), self, or consciousness, claiming this is everything and all pervasive. The more we separate this spirit through the individual mind, into duality or dichotomies, the greater the likelihood there will be disturbances in our existence. If we wish for fulfilment in life, to be centered in oneness, we must not separate, as energy is indivisible and common to all. This has been attributed to Brahma, the god of creation.

The second stage is self-awareness. Our actions should not be directed solely for our own benefit, but as *karma yoga* (selfless action), with love and compassion towards one and all. Here we raise our consciousness toward that *Brahman* (energy) that encompasses all. In doing so, there is less separation into this and that, for your self-interest. Selfless action is the supreme method of bringing all closer to the one. Consciousness on its own is nothing. It is merely self-consciousness. It defines what we are and sums us up. It is awareness that awakens the mind to the consciousness of oneself in unity with the universe. This stage attributes to Lord Krishna, the preserver.

As long as our awareness remains witness to the mind, the consciousness stays pure. But when it merges with our thoughts or desires and dualities in self-identification, separateness comes in and our consciousness dilutes into ego-consciousness. The mind should always be observant and alert proactively, to capture awareness in spontaneity. Eastern scriptures also describe various techniques to manifest extra energy through awareness.

Perception by the mind, on the other hand, is limited and differs from one individual to another. It is only from unlimited cosmic awareness, when one is awakened spiritually, that one can draw the energy to learn how to slow down the mind through various meditative, breathing and other practices. Thus begins a new journey in life. Now we can accumulate less materially, but be more fulfilled.

We transcend our thoughts and still the mind, to obtain fresh, pure energy through awareness. This is referred to as super consciousness or inner perception of the Self, the study of which is the focus of spiritualism.

The mind is designed to function mainly for its desires, in some way or the other, through the choices it makes. It relies on the conscious, subconscious and unconscious parts of the brain; it satiates its hunger in the present, while combining past and future thoughts and converting them into emotions that activate present motives. Emotions are our weakness. When combined with desire, we allow the mind to take control and become the victims of our circumstances, rather than the ones in control. This is where our personal power exhibits the results of our intentions.

In relation to the mind, happiness is a simple formula. If the mind gets what it wants, it is happy. Otherwise, it is not. It is a cycle of pleasure and pain. Is momentary happiness or pleasure the purpose of our lives? Are we to keep rotating and dancing in this vicious cycle of pleasure and pain? If we wish to go beyond these limited, narrow perceptions and thoughts, and this egoistic, materialistic life, we need to know the secret to perception of Self to understand super consciousness.

This book provides a glimpse into understanding spiritualism from a different perspective than the one most preachers and writers use. It emphasizes experiential realization rather than knowledge of spiritualism. It goes deeper than anything the mind can perceive, permeate or penetrate; harnessing cosmic energy, and changing from static to dynamic, in day-to-day living.

Super consciousness as a practice is far more relevant

today than it might have been thousands of years ago, when the sages explained it to their pupils. The reason is that the mind is designed primarily to look after itself. Humans alone have the unique power to discriminate and choose according to our own desires. However, when the mind goes beyond thoughts, towards silencing thoughts; and higher, toward witnessing its own self, we enter the realm of super consciousness. Now, we come to the third and most important stage.

After the mind has observed and understood a particular situation, we must silence it (its awareness, consciousness and everything we perceive), in order to enter a no-mind zone. Here, our actions must focus on knowing and understanding, accepting and surrendering, to everything in its totality. Our deeds, with reduced interference from the mind, become less prone to narrow self-centeredness or the ego, and more in tune with experiential realization.

One should keep in mind here, that no -mind zone in no way means 'thoughtlessness' or silencing the mind. Mind can never be silent for long; it can only slow down on its own accord when the energy of desire in self-interest reduces.

Thoughts are involuntary and a consequence of the degree of your self-consciousness with the interest involved in each situation. It can be further activated by the memory, turning into emotions and frenzy.

Even the term 'void' or 'nothingness' does not mean the mind is empty of all thoughts. It indicates that the mind is free from emotions and is less dependent on thoughts of external perceptions. In fact, nothing is everything, because it is only when you are nothing that 'Allness' emerges to exist.

Therefore, there is no 'void' or nothingness. The Self is fully aware of its presence as the Ultimate Reality, which by itself cannot be considered as void in any manner. It is more of the awareness in presence taking over the mind from external thoughts and aligning itself to all that exists as One. This is how thinkingness of the mind is replaced with 'knowingness'. Resistance by mind subsides; when thinkingness surrenders, it replaces that with alertness, watchfulness and awareness to culminate into knowingness.

This stage, if followed in the right manner, can lead us, with love for all and through selfless actions, towards that ultimate reality or oneness to which we all belong. We then merge duality with non-duality, positive with negative, God with Devil, and all that exists, with equal respect and grace, moving to a center where they become one, absolute and unified. This stage attributes to the cosmic god, Shiva.

It is here, Advaita emphasizes, that everything, being energy or self-in-continuum, is in the presence of only one, and there is no two. When we follow the self as a complete whole, in totality and not in separation, we can realize enlightenment or pure absolute energy. In accordance with this concept, when we exist in a life full of dualities, we experience life in a limited manner, with a bagful of happiness and sadness. We finally decompose and return to where we came from. But a very few, who have dedicated their lives wholly in devotion toward all that exists, never know the experience of happiness or sadness for themselves, but only the oneness all around them. Their lives, even after their bodies decompose, remain eternal.

This is what it means to realize God in everything there is; as present in all of us but waiting to be fulfilled. Buddhism deviates from the *Upanishads* in this respect. For Buddhists, life is an illusion, and there never was, nor will be, any *atman* or spirit. They believe one should not identify oneself with pure consciousness, as that is impossible and it remains unclear what happens when one realizes total awareness in *nirvana*.

In the final stage, as explained in the cycle of birth and death, the soul keeps wandering in multiple cycles of existence, passing from one to another so long as the individual self remains in isolation from its totality and the absolute unified cosmic consciousness. It can only relieve itself from this separation through absolute realization, with selfless actions or deeds in oneness, using the medium of love and devotion as its energy.

A person realizes enlightenment, meaning total awareness or pure consciousness, only when the soul is fulfilled, to live eternally. They are then conferred godhood – the answer to anyone who wishes to know: Who is God? God is always within and a part of us – but only in purity. We realize this eventually, through selfless deeds and numerous lives.

However, knowledge by itself is incomplete unless followed by action. Enlightened souls did not attain anything through knowledge but merged the body, mind and soul into the oneness of the universe. God is absolute and non-dual; present in all of us, but separated by the selfish actions of the mind. God cannot be attained through pursuit or seeking, only in the absoluteness of total acceptance – of good and bad – by simply surrendering to oneness and pure energy.

Advaita mentions non-duality as one, absolute, pure and total awareness – where there is nothing to attain but only to realize. In duality too, there is only one, but separated and stretched into opposites, away from their center. But because of our innate comprising of only energy, we cannot be divided, created or destroyed.

The *Upanishads* define God by clarifying we are all complete, as divinity is within us. We have to become aware, realize and fulfil this completeness.

Love, even though complete, as long as it remains in dual mode, is unfulfilled. The mind traps and places love into a cage of duality, cornering and separating it only for self, family and friends, with sentiments, attachments and prejudices, possessiveness and expectations. In such a case, love can turn into hate at any time, if all parameters concerning the individual self are not complied with. Love here is simply a transaction.

However, the moment love is free, the same spirit becomes pure and non-dual, flowing freely into that oneness where it belongs. Such love is absolute, to be shared and given to everyone, becoming the reason for the common phrase: Love is God. These words have such a deep meaning because, within all the other properties of energy, love is the only one that is never in 'wanting mode'. It fulfils when it parts and when we receive. That is why it is so closely related to, and conferred with God.

A child is complete in all respects, yet has to grow and finish the cycle of existence in that completeness in which he evolves physically and mentally, to fulfil his desires and purpose in life. This purpose continues in the cycle of birth and death, until he realizes the isolation in which he lives. From that completeness comes final oneness, in which he finally merges into completeness. This may take thousands of cycles of birth and death as the soul continues, in life, searching for that eventual fulfilment.

Non-duality in our existence is difficult to absorb, but then we rarely come across enlightened souls. How beautifully the Eastern sages explained the same thousands of years ago. Scientists are still researching such ancient mystical mysteries, and slowly coming to understand that we are nothing but pure spirit exhibiting dual properties while being part of an indivisible and indestructible whole. Science defines it as slow vibrational energy in human form.

Therefore, this complex phenomenon: God as everything, non-dual, all-pervasive, pure absolute energy; indestructible and indivisible, meaning it can neither be created nor destroyed. It just changes from one form to another, radiating, leaping and sparking in dual properties, in the form of existence, until that form reaches salvation.

Strangely, this intelligent energy manifests as awareness in human beings, in order to raise our consciousness to discover who we really are. *I am That*, God in purity and evil as its opposite. Individually, somewhere in-between, separated, we swing in godly or devilish acts, but continuing, with effort, to reach the center where the dual and non-dual dissolve into one.

The third stage, realizing *moksha* or liberation and becoming divine, after repeated cycles of birth and death, is a matter of belief. To repeat: soul or intelligent energy, after continuing into a new mind-body combination, in cycles of birth and death, is only fulfilled after reaching that stage of absoluteness or non-duality when the soul realizes liberation or enlightenment. Science still has a long way to go to decipher all these mystical connotations.

When the perceiver perceives the self,
arises the presence of consciousness
to witness what is being perceived.

Chapter 12
Am I What I Perceive?

WHAT ABOUT US AVERAGE MORTALS? We are gifts from the universe, manifesting pure, intelligent energy in the mind – from awareness into thoughts, emotions and reason – to perceive and enjoy this flow of life. So what if such average souls do not realize enlightenment? Our purpose should be to realize peace, love and harmony.

I perceive therefore I exist. Perception is necessary to declare my being. It is only through perception that I come to know my inner and outer Self. What constitutes my being is *'Brahman'* or energy. My inner being, as I understand, conforms to my mind as the witnessing Self, separate from the ego-self, and neither is it dependent nor has any gender.

Since it is beyond the perceptual thoughts, it is able to witness, observe and become aware of all that my mind does. It perceives my inner self, and remains aloof of all that my mind experiences. My mind perceives through its external perceptions via thoughts, in desires and attachments, but I am not that.

I am what I perceive through my series of experiences referred to as consciousness, settled in my sub-conscious or memory. The basis of memory clearly signifies that the experiencer and the 'rememberer' are indeed the same individual otherwise there can be no individual memory.

There must be some entity within our body and mind, who is witnessing our mind, who even observes during our sleep to make us conscious whether we have had a disturbed or a good sleep, and yet who is not affected by the three realms: illusions, empirical and the absolute reality. That witnessing Self in pure consciousness or the Awareness is who I am; the Perceiver.

I am that subject, in awareness, as the perceiver, perceiving through mind, the objects to be perceived. The cosmic beauty lies in the fact that I as the subject cannot know myself, until and unless I manifest with my mind, to know and experience the dichotomies through objects. For only then, my mind becomes aware to be conscious of what life is all about.

If I awaken to this Self-knowledge out of my ignorance that I can be aware and conscious of my own body and mind, it clearly proves that I can only be that awareness which defines my thoughts.

Simply put, I cannot observe my own self, as well as being the observer, unless the mind, through which I observe, dissolves into One in oneness and purity.

Therefore, I am that inner perceiver, the absolute energy, who is not a spectator but the experiencer, who is not the thinker, but the knower. I manifest into the mind, observing and watching, the inner me, the real me, experiencing and conscious. The more I participate through my abode, the mind, the more it flows, and this is made possible only when I am aware of my awareness in alertness.

At times, my mind separates more than it should, and is carried away in being overpowered by the external perceptions through desires and attachments. This turns me more into a spectator, watching helplessly my mind, so separated dancing and crying in dualities, shifting from the presence of my being into the past and future in thoughts of emotions. Then I perceive more through external perceptions, through my sensory organs into what existence has to offer.

The mind is so accustomed to external perceptions that it gets confused and puzzled when it cannot spectate, because during that period it is inner perception, which has taken over, in a higher awareness in participation of what it is keenly observing and watching in alertness. This is the difference between the mind, which perceives through thoughts and the consciousness perceiving through awareness.

In the beginning, the body and mind become instinctive in reacting to the probability of the experiencer. When this probability turns into an actuality, intuitiveness emerges through spontaneous manifestation of awareness in creativity. Here both the outer and the inner perceptions merge into one. This is how, when instincts from body and mind combines with spontaneous intuition it gives birth to intention, in order to continue and experience the flow of experiencing.

Intention is a direct phenomenon of the perceiver, the consciousness revealing exactly what and who you are. The external perception is more of a spectator, because it has to process the data which the mind has perceived through organs, trying to seek knowledge from the outside. The inner perceiver later comes into action, manifesting awareness from pure energy, to describe what the external has perceived. No amount of words, can really express and describe the reality behind any individual perceiver, or what goes through in the mind. It needs to be felt and experienced, which is always unique in each individual through his uniqueness.

The outward and the inward are not so different. They may have separated due to dualities in opposites, but definitely not divided into two.

They always function together, one externally and the other internally, depending which is more prominent over the other. They are one in reality, but only separated; more the separation, higher will be the anguish. That is why in spiritualism, you need to be concerned with both the inner and the outer, from rotating in their periphery, drawing them as close as possible towards their center.

It is only in the human mind that energy can manifest into the pure intelligence called awareness. Besides knowing who and what we are, it is also important to know *how* we are. How are we utilizing the special intelligent energy gifted to us? This answer, we need give only to ourselves and realize that man today is insensitive to all that is around him, remaining separated by a notion called ego.

We are chiefly interested in accumulating and consuming; concerned with our attachments. Hence, we remain separated from our source. We need to understand that the only way to attain peace and harmony is to flow in this current of life, accepting all situations in their totality, in togetherness or oneness, with all.

We know that duality and non-duality in existence are dichotomies or reference points, separated from their center; from the oneness to which we all belong. In this separation, an individual, after borrowing cosmic energy in spontaneous awareness, combines it with his thoughts to create his self-consciousness and decides how he wishes to flow in his existence. Either he creates a balance by drawing the two closer to their center, in surrender of ego, and in acceptance, love and totality; or remains separated in delusion or *Maya* and its apparent cycles of momentary pleasure and pain.

In spiritual seeking, enlightenment through external thoughts is intellectually impossible; it cannot be gained through knowledge or reading books. Only a select few out of millions and that too, after thousands of years, have realized enlightenment. Such realization is beyond the mind and thoughts – it is purely experiential, through deeds. Hence, my repeated references to shining examples like Buddha and Jesus, who realized such enlightenment.

Many spiritual writers have become dejected with the search for non-duality and spiritual enlightenment; with nothing new, they feel the search has been futile. Many books have been written on the subject with such incomplete knowledge. My answer is: *there is nothing to seek, achieve or get.* The point is to understand and live towards a non-dual way. Therefore, there is no reason to be dejected, frustrated or exhausted. The contention of many writers: live in the now and plunge into unconditional love. While all there is to it is just this and not that, the essence of life lies in understanding both as the force of life in a single, composite unit.

First, all that exists is definitely energy. How we acquire knowledge and awareness of what that is, is important to know *how* to live in peace and harmony. We are often told that whatever there is, exists in the now. Yes! There is only the now, for the past and future exist only in the mind. Every moment happens in the present.

However, as we have come to realize, the mind can never capture the now, so when we leave the mind, we are in the now; we live from one moment to the next. When the mind thinks, time turns that into the past and future; by the time the mind recaptures the now, a new one has taken its place. We require awareness of the present from one moment to the next. We have to know the difference between dual and non-dual existence, for duality is only in the mind. In addition, we must be aware of how spirit becomes aware in the form of non-dual energy in order to align the two.

Moreover, unconditional love is not something the mind can conceive of. Love is an experience, to be experienced beyond the mind and time, in its own presence. It is a characteristic of non-duality in being pure, absolute and divine. Love becomes dual only in its conditionality in our minds, through its relativity to hate.

It becomes imperative that if we wish to harmonize our lives, we need to obtain self-knowledge, become self-aware, and then be in self-realization – not to seek but to be able to transcend in experiential realization. Therefore, combining all the knowledge of science, psychology and spirituality becomes necessary not to attain anything, but to experience and realize who and what we are, and how we are to exist.

I repeat again, so you will remember that now can never be captured by the mind, only experienced. Neither time nor the mind can stop or become still in the now. Time keeps ticking away. Neither is the mind designed to perform in the now; it is completely dependent on the past or thinking of the future; it can only experience the present moment in relation to its past and anxiety about its future. Concentration and transcendental meditation may slow down the activity of the mind, or temporarily take the mind away from the past and the future, but even then, experience of the now will only register in the past tense in the mind.

In the mind, the past creates the present, which further influences the future. It is the awareness of the now, spontaneously, that is important. If we are alert and observant, we will notice later how fresh intelligence intuitively and creatively enters our being as choice-less spontaneous energy, providing the impetus for us to improve our thoughts and rise in intelligence.

Therefore, more than just being in the now live from one moment to the next. In addition, when we hear, 'Let everything be as it is, because this is as this is', that may not be the answer. It is today and each moment that we need to be concerned about. It is today that is in our hands – to be proactive, work hard and deliver results – for nobody knows what may unfold tomorrow. On the other hand, tomorrow may never come.

I am what I perceive – this is our reality, through inner perceptions. Existence is normally experienced in sensory terms because without the perceiver, nothing remains, neither apparent nor real. Because of the duality of existence, life brings both joy and grief. Even reality is what we perceive and observe.

Our purpose should be to acquire Self-knowledge in awareness, in order to practice Self-realization. Not in order to achieve something spectacular or become enlightened, but to align the spirit with the actions of the body and mind, and so realize a more fruitful life. We need to become more sensitive to all, because love in duality is restricted to self, family and friends, inviting sorrow, jealousy and grief. We must realize how, when we can see the same self in others, our own self becomes pure in unison with all. We cannot live in exclusion; it is only in this oneness that we can receive greater joy and bliss from our apparent existence.

As for God, the faith of many generations keeps reminding us that there has to be some infinite perceiver, above or beyond, guiding and preventing us from falling into utter darkness. This is something we may have felt a number of times, in various circumstances when faith, logic and reason fail but some Supreme Force comes to protect us.

However, Self-knowledge and the nature of consciousness teach us otherwise. Be aware and realize that God is within; it requires an awakening from the bondage of suffering this and that. It keeps reminding us to liberate ourselves from this ignorance of duality and become pure in total awareness.

Body and mind are like waves in an ocean; they come, go, and decompose, having no permanent reality of their own. In such existence, there is a realm of consciousness, in limited space and time, so long as we are there; perceiving objects and the world as manifestations of who we really are – essence of the Absolute. Before the emergence of consciousness, there is no duality, time or space. There is no separation, no distinction or identification, nor is there body and mind. For consciousness is the basic fact of life, to experience duality and realize non-duality.

In reality, we are that pure presence, beyond our limited perceptions, unaware of its awareness. We do not even know our real existence unless consciousness comes along in body-mind to reveal its true identity. Consciousness is the experience that comes and goes, existing in duality. Within that, we perceive ourselves as body-mind: our world.

The sun does not know of its existence. It just gives out light, for like you, it is singular and non-dual. As rays of light reveal the presence of the sun objectively, in the same manner, consciousness reveals our objective presence through our perceptions. The mind, through perception, dictates initial understanding and consciousness of what we are, providing a sense of being and awareness of who we are.

Awareness is *who* we are; consciousness proclaims *what* we are and perceptions through the body-mind complex reflect *how* we are. Non-duality is the substratum in which consciousness comes and goes, having no independent reality. Just as we cannot exist without consciousness, in the same way awareness or absolute reality cannot exist or manifest without body and mind.

When the perceiver perceives the self, there arises the presence of consciousness, as witness to what is being perceived. It is that state of absoluteness, manifesting through awareness that by itself cannot arise in the un-manifested energy of the universe. This way, a seeker disappears in his spiritual seeking, realizing there is nothing to seek of that absoluteness; telling us what we seek is already what we are.

Therefore, as we exist in a dual existence, be watchful of the mind. Be alert, be aware, and restrict choices to understanding, accepting, indulging, outgrowing and transforming oneself.

Create a balance or center, from which we can be proud in awareness of our real presence in this universe. Life will be natural this way, with less fear and anxiety and more freedom; informing us that belief in the separated self is the cause of all sufferings.

Spiritualism is going beyond thoughts of a separated mind into thoughts of a unified consciousness, in order to witness by perceiving that awareness telling us who, what and how we really are.

This is how I try to live my life, witnessing my thoughts and going with the flow; accepting both positive and negative with equal grace and respect; being more concerned with how and what I am doing in this existence rather than its outcome. May God bless us all!

*Happiest are those who have the temperament
to accept sadness.*

CHAPTER 13
CENTRING

TO BE CENTRED IN SPIRITUALISM is to become alive; to reach a point where intellect and awareness dissolve, empowering us to focus and concentrate our energies toward fulfilment. Centring becomes the source of vitality from which life radiates; the mind is no longer a wanderer and we become composed.

This is a very interesting subject, in which we come to know that the mind has a habit of taking over control, ruling through desires, attachments and emotions. Through specific meditative methods, the mind is to be tamed, which may alter our lives completely. Through such methods, we are able to use the mind as an instrument, witnessing all its weaknesses and the games it plays, living from moment to moment in awareness, rather than emotions dictating the mind. If practiced with sincerity and dedication, these methods change one's life, bringing both magnanimity and equanimity.

All of us are centered in some way or the other, in our minds through our egos, in our hearts through emotions, and in our bodies through our stomachs. But there are other subtle centring practices discussed in the ancient texts of India that were later elaborated upon in deeper detail by the Buddha, as well as the Greeks and various other civilizations.

Centring is important because the mind is incapable of realizing the ultimate, and this book is all about knowing the secret of what the ultimate reality is. The mind definitely becomes the deciding factor due to its capacity for thinking, but because of personal limitations, we need to focus and centralize. How can we still the mind, go beyond and focus toward its center rather than its periphery, in order to realize its role beyond desire? The five senses of the body, which provide data to the mind, need a central point at which to dissolve. Otherwise, the mind will keep chattering in the self-centeredness of its own ego, attached to comforts and materialism.

We may represent centring as a triangle, with each point containing an aspect of the mind: the witnessing mind, the perceptive mind and the experiential mind. They all converge toward the center point to create our uniqueness, through mindfulness.

Centring brings in focus and concentration, thus not allowing the mind to rule over our thoughts through self-interest and emotions. It takes us into that spiritual realm where the mind becomes a witness to all that is happening, going beyond body-mind into that center of reality, where there is only oneness in a unified consciousness.

This center then becomes a link between the universe and us. The navel as a center is one we are born with, being the original connection to one's mother and the universe. Then the mind has its center in the ego through intellect; and the heart in its feelings through emotions. There is another center, which the ancient scriptures strongly consider – the space between our inhalation and exhalation. Breathing is also the link between the inner and outer self. It is that mechanism of life, which brings us to a sense of being alive, quietly saying, 'I am your life'.

When we shift the centers of the mind and heart towards breathing, we come into the present; the mind stills and the heart slows down. The three are in unison. We are in the now. However, in order to function, the mind has to desire, so the mind, becomes linked to the past and the future. The ego restricts the center only to the desires and attachments with the self. Moreover, in order for someone to be in the now, to attain that, the mind needs to cease its thoughts of past and future, which is not possible.

Do not think of now, only experience it, because *now* is that divine act or truth that makes us who we are, that creates our tomorrow. Always remember, unless knowledge is lived and experienced, it is nothing but ego, taking us towards anger, anxiety and frustration. In the same manner, truth resides far from the mind; it is purely experiential and existential, manipulated and exaggerated by the mind; truth (or love, for that matter), can be present only in the now; whereas the mind is never in the now.

This chapter is dedicated more on how to do than doing. It deals with motion or movement. Life is nothing but movement, ideas or thought; everything in the body and mind is in motion until we die. Even in stillness, there are movements of experience, even when thoughts or consciousness is not there (such as in deep sleep or zero movement). Centring represents the motion that directs our energy to focus on any required movement. How to focus, concentrate and optimize the usage of this movement is what we are concerned about, because they are sources of influence to the body, mind and spirit.

Energy is constantly moving, simultaneously leaping and sparking in waves and particles in any subatomic field, represented as gross (body), subtle (Mind), and the core (thoughts and consciousness).

The frequency of the vibrations, requires motion to bring it alive. Harnessing this motion of energy in the right direction is of relevance here and so desperately needed: how to align body, mind and spirit in our daily lives.

I have provided centring practices for you to ponder and consider. However, before that I would like to elaborate on two ancient Eastern philosophies on centring. Originating from the same country, both lead us towards the same goal. With the passage of time, however, both philosophies, after distancing themselves from India and going towards China, became contradictory in their approaches. The debate between them makes the subject even more interesting, capturing the meaning in a better way, so we can form our own opinions.

The difference is in how each philosophy treats the subject of awareness. The *Upanishads*, *Vedas* and *Tantra*, all speak the same language, about awareness being the source of everything. Our body and mind are nothing but decomposable energy that returns to where it came from. However, life is total awareness, and that is who we really are. The higher our level of awareness, the purer is our consciousness in living. It is in awareness that we exist and experience, making all efforts to live a life of integration and syntropy, despite the disorder or entropy of our chaotic and separated mind in dualities. However, Shunyu Suzuki, the Zen philosopher, emphasizes effort with effortlessness rather than effort with awareness.

The first English text on centring appeared in 1918 and was introduced to the Western world by Paul Reps. He is the only one to mention both these philosophies in one text. In the Foreword to his book, *Zen Flesh, Zen Bones* (1957), referring to pre-Zen writings, says; *Centring, a transcription of ancient Sanskrit manuscripts, first appeared in the spring 1955 issue of Gentry magazine, New York. It presents in ancient teaching, still alive in Kashmir and parts of India after more than four thousand years that may well be the roots of Zen.* The first chapter on centring notes: *Zen is nothing new, neither is it anything old. Long before Buddha was born the search was on in India, as the present work shows.*

As an addendum to *Zen Flesh, Zen Bones*, Reps gives the first English translation of the *Vigyan Bhairav Tantra*, which describes 112 meditation methods (*tantras* or centring techniques). This *tantra* is an ancient teaching from India, written over 5000 years ago. He probably may have noticed the differences in the two philosophies but did not comment on them. Several other translations and explanations of the *tantras* are available, including Bettina Bäumer's *Vijnana Bhairava: The Practice of Centring Awareness* (2007), and Dmitri Semenov's *Vijnanabhairava or Techniques for Entering Liminal Consciousness* (2010). Osho in The Book of Secrets provides the most exhaustive explanation.

Zen, according to Wikipedia, is a school of Mahayana Buddhism, which originated in China during the 6th century as Chan (Chinese translation of the Indian word *dhyana*, meaning 'to meditate'). Zen meditation has become a popular tool in the Western world today. Shunyu Suzuki, who founded San Francisco Zen Center, he has been credited with being the person to bring this philosophy to the West through his book, *Zen Mind, Beginner's Mind* (1970). It has become a Western spiritual classic.

The meditation technique Suzuki emphasizes in his book is 'effortless effort', based on breathing techniques (*pranayama*) given in the *tantric* and *Upanishads*. However, he differs on the subject of awareness. Let us compare the two styles and conclude on their efficacy with an open mind, since both techniques are based upon centring. Suzuki tells us: *We must make some effort, but we must forget ourselves in the effort we make. In this realm, there is no subjectivity or objectivity. Our mind is just calm, **without any awareness.** In this unawareness, every effort and every idea and thought will vanish. [...] You should keep your mind on your breathing until you are not aware of your breathing.*

The philosophies clash in their ideologies. They speak in different languages, but the subject is the same. One speaks about a method in which effort in awareness is the essence; the other says to forget oneself in the effort, and that the action should be only in effortlessness. The first says all effort should be done in awareness, whereas in Zen, as per Suzuki, there should be calmness without awareness. Both methods place great emphasis on breathing, but in *tantras* one needs to be aware of breath, while Suzuki negates this awareness.

Effortlessness, according to Suzuki, is to act without any struggle; with the act coming from the inner realm to present who you are, and to acknowledge the natural flow of your presence. Whereas in the *tantras*, any act to reach uniform flow or become effortless, requires awareness.

Effortless flow comes naturally only after practice in creating that awareness in the subconscious. Initially, there is resistance to any act; we are to make effort in order to gain momentum, and only after achieving that momentum in awareness, does effort reduce. Thereafter the subconscious takes over, and the same becomes an effortless act. I would suggest, one should switch focus to some other action, if results are not achieved even after all effort and awareness have been applied, to back it up.

Today, technology is gradually improving every product for our usage with the least expenditure of effort. However, technology deals with mechanical products, whereas we are so unique from one another that the style of movement naturally differs. Therefore, strong effort, awareness and endeavor, are all intrinsic to the initiation of any action. If it does not become effortless with the passage of time and experience, it is not worth the act.

An individual, depending on his intelligence, alertness and spontaneous awareness (intuitiveness), is bound to select only those acts that require the least effort; his mind, on autosuggestion, tells him when, what and how to choose which act. This awareness has been considered as our own uniqueness.

Certain methods or techniques in the art of centring are provided in the next chapter, so that we can enable the spirit to move towards that oneness to which we belong. They may seem simple on first reading, but as we practise, experience and realize them, substantial effort and determination of the spirit, in awareness, is required, rather than of the mind. We then begin to act subconsciously, more in the knowing, doing and experiencing, than in the mind's thinking, brooding or choosing of good and bad.

Centring is a path by which energies flow to unite, focus and gain strength or concentrate on any subject. Breathing as a process has been given a lot of importance in meditation and yoga. Centring is a process that can be controlled voluntarily or remain an involuntary act. In learning this method of meditative breathing, we can balance the autonomic nervous system, affect the pressure on the heart and relax a disturbed mind. It is a powerful method and the only function of the body that can be performed consciously and unconsciously.

We require centring because the mind is never stationary at any given point. It is always moving here and there, into this and that. The brain is like any other part of the body, whereas the mind is moving in the brain. When we centralize awareness in our thoughts, the content becomes our consciousness. The mind is pure movement, and through the centring process, consciousness takes over and navigates the mind. Awareness is the context from which consciousness becomes the content of the mind.

Similarly, meditation and breathing are centring techniques that help dissolve the overactive mind to a point where we are thrown into the center. Instead of the mind leaping here and there, thinking various external thoughts in desire and attachment, we become centered in our own presence of being.

As mentioned earlier, energy is constantly moving; it needs to be controlled and centralized to obtain the right experience in any human action. Each individual has a different experience, and this effort can be accomplished only by self-effort. Religion, science and gurus do not really mention experiential realization; their concern is more with theory, books and lectures. Where methods, techniques and curative processes are provided, even though each case remains different, they are only general examples.

Each of us has a different experience in any situation, just as medicines have different effects on different people, though the dosage remains the same. Similarly, the spirit takes us towards a different experience or realization. Spiritualism is the art of centring, but its realization is experiential; there is more learning in doing rather than in theory. Not even Buddha or Jesus could describe or preach his or her own enlightenment to anyone. They could only provide methods; effort and adaptation are different in each individual case.

Just as energy is movement, centering too is movement of energy to a point at which it becomes stronger or greater. Our individuality or personal power is our center – out of various multi-centers and multi-dimensional energies – all combining into one path. Breathing with awareness is one of the best-known centring methods. Even though it flows unconsciously, when we learn the art of centring or conscious breathing in awareness, we obtain the first results in self-realization.

When awareness is aware of the observer,
observing what is being observed;
When awareness is aware of its reality;
it is not separated into dichotomy.
Only then conflicts dissolve in a realization of oneness.

CHAPTER 14
CENTRING WITH AWARENESS

WISDOM NORMALLY COMES WITH AGE. When we are young, we centralize and focus our activities and energies into our ambitions. The experience of those results matures later; we tend to become more silent rather than speak of our personal experiences. For that matter, experiences too, can only be expressed partially, depending on our level of intelligence. However, the sum total of our experiences definitely can largely be felt or observed by others through our individuality.

To a highly knowledgeable person, centring techniques are often not that important; his ego urges him to think he knows it all. The problem arises when the mind confuses knowledge with experience. This is very common and most knowledgeable people advise others on methods they have never practiced or experienced. However, no knowledge is complete unless experienced; otherwise, it only helps to inflate the ego. Never be convinced that knowledge is complete or the ultimate answer to everything.

Knowledge is only a method to experience knowing, doing, and realizing any subject. The teaching may remain the same, but its effect or result on a particular person differs. Experience is deeply personal; no single solution or teaching can fully suffice. That is why there are so many failures when any process or technique is generalized. Centring methods, chosen for the individual, are one way that have succeeded.

In centring, there are certain fundamental steps we need to remember, follow and practice. We have to be alert to understand every action through knowledge and past awareness; be highly observant to be spontaneous and intuitive, to imbibe fresh awareness;

and then accept both positive and negative with equal respect. Without discriminating or choosing, we should accept both dualities gracefully; indulge, experience, and then outgrow what we do not prefer. This way, one attains transformation by using the mind but at the same time not allowing it to interfere, separate or become emotional. The mind should be given importance only until the stage of observing and knowing any subject. After that, during the stage of acceptance and immersion, spontaneity, knowing and awareness should take over so that one can experience, outgrow and transform while totally focused on the subject at hand.

In centring the mind is in totality and acceptance, things we have done do not drop away effortlessly. However, we do not need to make an effort to shun, renounce or give up anything. Those who transcend by accepting both good and bad at the same time remain centered; unfavorable things drop away automatically, just as when an electric light is switched on, darkness disappears on its own. We are then free from the mind, to connect with that oneness in freedom and love what it has to offer.

This is where acceptance, as an act of centring, plays its role. We need to understand that what is happening to 'me' is the same for others as well. If I justify or condemn, others will do the same; acceptance is required to harmonize such a situation. Acceptance purifies our energy and changes it into love. Right or wrong are two sides of the same coin; there is no need to separate them into two, for they are joined at their center, each having some value. Separated, they become lost in their own identity.

When the mind is not centered, our life becomes purposeless. We are happy when we get something and unhappy when we do not. If we are centered, the mind is focused on our purpose with joy and peace – which is far greater than creating conflicts in life. Therefore, I repeat this below, systematically, for further clarification.

Spiritual Methods Of Centring

Unlike science, spiritualism is concerned only with knowing and living with the clarity that all that exists is but a manifestation of oneness. For spiritualism is simply awareness in spontaneity rather than the mind's unique style of discriminating, choosing and separating each object from its subject in self-centeredness.

In spiritualism, awareness transforms the intellect and its reasoning to a higher level of wisdom, followed by sensitivity towards compassion; ending with completeness. In this, no books, literature, religious or spiritual gurus can remove the suffering, anxiety and despair, which exist despite wealth and comfort. Awareness needs to be cultivated from within, by our own self in our own uniqueness, in order to reach the completeness required by spirituality.

The first step is to be observant and alert from one moment to the next, making this a habit; only then will we be competent enough to capture the creative, intuitive, imaginative awareness in spontaneity, before the mind can interfere to convert this fresh energy into thoughts of duality. Our effort should be accompanied with awareness in spontaneity.

The second step is to accept any situation in its totality, by not allowing the mind to discriminate and choose with a bias towards our likes and dislikes. That way we are able to accept both positive and negative as one, with equal grace and respect, knowing and understanding any situation with acceptance and totality. In spiritual living, we are to behave and act as animals do – with limited use of the perceptive and discriminatory mind but in complete sync with nature, just as a bee goes from one flower to another in awareness, spontaneously selecting without much effort or emotion, and deciding on one instantaneously.

The third step, after making that spontaneous effort in awareness to confront any situation with acceptance and totality, we should participate wholeheartedly, in complete mindfulness, from one moment to another, in order to absorb, focus, concentrate and live that moment. In this sort of indulgence we are bound to effortlessly disapprove, when the mind is not discriminating, what we do not like and outgrow it to transform into something better. In this manner, we are bound to to allow our inner experiences with that spontaneity of mind, reducing thoughts, as we continue to exist, surrendering our ego and replacing it with acceptance of all/any situation.

Perceptive thinking, from our senses, releases concentrated mental and physical energy, which has properties of disintegration, depending on the egoistic, emotional force of the self-centeredness. This may be practical for materialistic living, but it is damaging to the body, mind and soul, eventually leading to conflicts, anxiety and suffering. In order to balance this, there is spiritual thinking in the spontaneity of the now, in awareness, in which, unlike with the mind, we do not predict by calculating benefits. The same awareness integrates with the environment in totality and accepts its reality, in harmony.

In such a spiritual method of living, we are centered, alive and closer to the oneness, in integration and completeness, and our perceptive thoughts of knowledge and understanding merge with creative thoughts in action, with the spontaneity of now. Imagine how peaceful existence would be if we reduced the anxiety of unnecessarily thinking about things that have yet to take place or trying to prove that we are smarter than others, when all we really need to do is realize that creative, intuitive and imaginative energy is hidden within us.

Another method that is normally applied in spiritual living is a meditative one. Again, this has to do with improving and transforming awareness to a higher level of wisdom, giving rise to completeness and compassion towards the oneness; that spiritualism is all about us. Cosmic awareness leads us towards cosmic consciousness.

Here, the first step is to be prepared to accept any situation, positive or negative, and not let the mind tell us what to do only in self-interest. In choosing what we should and should not do, we should not take shelter or refuge in any outside source, but promote thinking inward into that awareness within us. Do not allow the ego to give excuses and explanations. Remember that the last person we know in this world is our own self, because the mind in its self-centeredness will not let us do so. In this manner, instead of our biased thoughts choosing between this and that, our action in acceptance should be more in awareness than from excitement or agitation. To repeat: remember that good/bad, positive/negative, truth/untruth are just symptoms of the self-interested mind. In reality or in awareness, these dualities simply get subsumed into one.

The second step is to observe, contemplate and always be alert to whether any faith, self-interest, dogma or mental hesitancy is detrimentally blocking such investigation.

The third step, after this awakening, is to accept the reality of any situation using the intellect and our reason, not by questioning but in acceptance. Questioning in self-interest is necessary for our material world, but here we are discussing how to reduce excitement, agitation and turbulence in the mind. We must exercise effort in awareness from one moment to the next in consonance with the subject, without caring too much about its outcome or result. This method enables us to utilize our power of awareness from moment to moment, with a serene and peaceful mind. Our psychic energies attract cosmic energy in providing us with the fulfilment we seek.

The reality of any situation is in the balance and centring of dualities with the purpose of living a wholesome life, in awareness. Spiritualism requires the merging of worldly and spiritual living in the right essence; where there is total acceptance, devotion and love in what we do. Both existences are necessary, because the basic requisites of living, as given in the *Upanishads*, are clearly stated through the process of *dharma, artha, kama* and *moksha*: with our own values of righteousness, we must first secure financial stability to fulfil worldly and sensual desires; our path eventually culminating in spiritual realization or liberation (*moksha*).

In existence, we live an egocentric life, more concerned with the accumulation of wealth and knowledge, bothered about what others think of us, and how much we can exhibit our superiority over others. When exhausted, due to either age or saturation in materialism, we start thinking about self-actualization, to become aware of our consciousness. Then we realize the trap of duality, the reason for our anxiety, despair, depression and loneliness. We find that our minds have become victims of circumstance, always discriminating, choosing, cutting and dividing with our likes and dislikes, getting into conflicts rather than being in control and centered within our own selves.

Do not try to suppress anger, lust or jealousy; just let them be. Accept but be aware; otherwise, these emotions will become strong enough to pull us in deeper. Through acceptance in observing self or indulging in awareness with experience, we can transform gradually, be able to withdraw from whatever we may not approve of, transcending beyond, to where we are wise rather than merely knowledgeable. This way we do not change anything. We remain the same; we have merely acted in accordance with our circumstance and not using the mind to discriminate, choose, justify or judge between one thing and another. It is better to be aware through existential experience and acceptance.

In a similar manner, we will not knowingly do things that are wrong; evaluating, comparing or justifying and then acting. Separating the mind through duality is not going to make it any better. It may personally give us more benefits, but in the end it will separate us from others if we are in the shadow of narrow-mindedness. Similarly, never suppress the ego; otherwise, it will just grow bigger without our even realizing it. Instead, exercising the ego through observation, awareness and acceptance, will begin to dissolve it, making it easier for us to see the other side of the fence, where love is waiting to draw closer to us.

Accept the self, the way we are is in itself, a centring method. Then try to change the mind, because the mind is designed to think we are good and others are bad. When the mind is angry, we justify. However, when someone else is angry, we criticize. This way the mind retains the habit of keeping us away from truth and reality. This sort of double standard, justifying that we are right and the others wrong, is bound to cause disturbances in life.

If each of us starts to think we are better than the others, constantly defending our points of view, society as a whole is bound to remain in chaos. That is exactly what is happening today with individuals, societies and countries; each is defending its own perception of what is right. Therefore, it means that no one is wrong.

Right and wrong exist as parts of a whole; there is no need to separate them. By accepting both, the mind starts to change; what we dislike, we will withdraw from, without thinking, and begin experiencing only what is good for us; not comparing, condemning or justifying. In this way, we transform ourselves into the totality of any subject at hand, rather than perceiving it objectively and emotionally.

Observe the difference in life when we accept and experience with awareness, alertness and observation, as compared to when we evaluate or justify, acting mainly for self-benefit. This, in itself, is a choice we make, between the former or latter.

The former is considered to be proactive, meaning to act before our thoughts materialize on the subject; and the latter is to be reactive, when thoughts take center stage.

Take for example the case of greed: we know it is there, and our overwhelming desire (say for money or sex), is driving us crazy. Everyone is bound to point out the negative aspects and the harm such obsession is likely to cause. However, if we follow the methods given here, we can accept gracefully the overpowering intensity of such desires and alertly observe our own behavior. We gradually become aware of our overindulgence and our common sense and reason begin to guide us, reminding us that anything in the extreme is detrimental. The mind starts changing, unquestioningly and in silence, with the inner, intuitive force of awareness, psychologically reducing our urges. Without any further interference from the mind, we can transform in totality, with no need to reject anything.

Another example is smoking. We all know it is injurious to health. Yet the smoker's body demands nicotine, and the mind says: 'so what, and who cares?' We can continue to indulge and so harm ourselves knowingly. Even if we force ourselves to stop, by various mind techniques or other methods, we still fail, simply because suppression of any desire multiplies the urge, and soon enough we revive the old habit. However, if we begin to observe ourselves meditatively, with alertness, we can become inwardly aware of every act we do.

Gradually, in such awareness, we can wean ourselves off the cigarettes that once controlled the mind through addiction – through sheer awareness, common sense and inner reasoning. This transforms us and we move away from that situation with grace, acceptance, and in totality, giving us no reason to suppress any urge. All we need to do is allow our inner power to reason with the mind in awareness, where our subconscious, with its own past understanding of the good and bad effects of smoking, will guide our power of reason by effortlessly rejecting what we do not approve of. In this manner, the mind, which promotes our self-interest, ego, attachments and desires, takes a back seat and is unable to control and influence us.

Take another case of centring - fasting. The West is more concerned with the physical aspect of fasting and the benefits of detoxification. The East, today, overcomes any guilt by fasting and not eating non-vegetarian fare for a day or so and adhering to the stricter diet prescribed by religion.

Tantra says fasting is an act of contemplation, discipline and meditation in awareness. While fasting, we are less excited and agitated, more silent, eat less and the mind slows down. This state of mind readies us, in awareness, for something better. In ancient times, seers would contemplate and meditate in order to silence the chattering mind in order to activate inner perception and achieve communion with the witnessing self.

We realize the reason our minds play with us; minds that are supposed to be instruments but which have turned into our masters, making us dance to our own narrow, self-minded approach, mingled with emotion. The reason for this is that the mind, like science and religion, is bound to separate one duality from another. The mind is only for our self-interest at the expense of everything else and makes us feel jealous and destructive.

Transcending such dualities and centring the two in oneness, is the process and meaning of spiritualism.

Duality is to exist; non-duality is divine.
In the centre is that oneness
From which they are separated.

CHAPTER 15
CENTRE OF LIFE

LIFE BRINGS US TO A CROSSROAD where, in sheer exasperation, we may say, 'Enough is enough!' We are not going to keep yo-yoing on this seesaw of the mind, bouncing from one end to another, from one duality to another, when we are not the judges of what is right or not. Besides, something good for one person may be detrimental for another, clearly demonstrating the hollowness of life. Is growth just the accumulation of assets, of wealth, and about materialism? At times we may wonder why, even after attaining knowledge, wealth and friends, we are still unhappy.

There has to be something beyond the mind, since we still feel lonely in spite of possessing the things money can buy, the love of friends and family, and good health. Happiness, in such cases, is short-lived and seems to fly away in a jiffy, leaving us once again in the same world of me and mine. In short, we are off-centered, leading a false life of attaining comforts and having no understanding of contentment, peace and happiness. Here, happiness is by the mind purely as what it receives; if it does not get something, we enter a state of unhappiness.

Existential reality is being aware of that presence of our being, in the now. Whereas, experiential reality demands that extra inner perception or higher consciousness to indulge in acceptance and transform. In this circle of evolving body-mind-soul, the former two rely upon sensory perceptions and the latter on awareness. Through our continuous experiences, inner and outer, our consciousness develops to form this circle. The periphery of the circle consists of physical, mental, social, emotional and financial realms. Spiritual energy consolidates all these in a center, forming its own domain through our common sense, intention and individuality. Wellness and joy depend on the inter-relatedness of the inner and outer dimensions, with spiritual awareness balancing all in the right perspective.

This is when we must learn to alter our lifestyle and focus our energies on totality and unison rather than separation – the cause of all misery. We reach a stage where our present goes beyond thoughts and constant demands for accumulation and comforts. We feel the need to evolve, and transform deep within; to converge and centralize those energies into acceptance. A feeling of surrender arrives, not to anyone else but to our own ego, in such totality that the mind is in balance. There is calmness and poise in the midst of our universal energy and the music of oneness and awareness, rather than centered in thoughts, like a slave to incessant desires.

This holds true for all of us. This sort of balance will bring us to the center point from which we will be able to observe the mind functioning like a witness, without being directly involved in any situation. We will accept happiness and sorrow on equal terms, automatically shunning whatever does not suit us. We will then be able to tell the mind that happiness and sadness are two sides of the same coin. We will be prepared to face and accept any consequence that may arise from our acts and deeds, good or bad.

On the other hand, the mind will keep demanding and wanting more and more, causing vicissitudes, presenting all sorts of obstacles. To balance this, nature has taught us how to be aware of the present moment, to focus, concentrate, and accept whatever comes our way. We must experience and realize this through mindfulness, rather than a narrow mind, deviously thinking about only how to cut and divide.

This way, we can act and feel different, and be more with the self rather than surrounded by an illusory world, where everything changes according to the whims and fancies of the mind. We will live more for the self, rather than to prove to others who and what we are. We will start to enjoy our own company, awaken toward that center where separation decreases, conflicts reduce, gaps disappear, and acceptance of the laws of nature prevails in the mind, with no need to defy everything that presents itself. We become more silent as we change, and the mind shifts its focus. In this way, we can live more existentially, in tune with nature, of which we are a part.

This silence is being in tune with totality; it is not forced upon us. This calmness is our nature, attained through acceptance rather than transcendental meditation. We have reached the center where everything is happening, and we are observing, accepting, being proactive in totality, rather than reacting to situations. Everything happens in complete acceptance and surrender to that oneness in which we all belong. We have no need to adjust and alter our energies to suit the ego, or to react in any manner after analyzing and calculating how we may benefit more than others may. We have thus learned to accept both negative and positive, as two separated ends of the same completeness.

In this way, a deep connection develops between reality and totality in any situation; a contentment that lingers in harmony and silence. We have been transformed into oneness rather than living only for oneself. This center is our reality; the rest is purely an interpretation of the mind. As we know, the mind separates existence into two; that is its only job. The mind is superior to that of all other living creatures because it knows how to discriminate and choose. With this power of choice, the mind generally remains in reaction mode, never in the now, always analyzing its self-interest and desire, taking us away from reality.

This is the reason I have never been able to understand the relationship between the mind and the now. I keep hearing and reading about the power of now, being in the now, as everything is in the now. For me, life is movement and energy is always moving. Truth, love or realities take place in the now, but not in the mind. We may experience them from one moment to the next, but when the mind captures the now, it turns everything into dualities of this and that. Then we are mixed up in truth, lies, love, jealousy, hatred, etc. If an experience by the mind is narrated, various people in any situation tell it differently.

If we seek peace, we need to stay away from the mind, to remain in the present – full of awareness, choice-less, alert, lost in the experience of now. Through this presence, we become aware of the now. It loses its essence when the mind takes over. The presence is awareness. The way *nirvana* is total awareness, now is pure, absolute and complete; like truth and love, they cannot be perceived by the mind. By being alert and observant, we may obtain a flash of this intuitive and creative energy in an attentive and choice-less manner, bringing us into the reality that the presence is all about.

Our presence should be in mindfulness, a place where we live from one moment to another existentially, being and concentrating, in full awareness of the moment. Mindfulness is living in the present, where we are not affected by the mind with sorrows about the past, anxiety about the future; or excitement about the present. Mindful living is living one moment to another in deep acceptance and awareness. This is our reality.

Reality is always one and remains the same, whereas the mind can never remain constant. In order to exist, the mind needs to discriminate, define and relate to something else. It is in relation to coldness that we define heat; otherwise, it loses its relevance. Let the mind do its job; evil is required to be able to give birth to good; lies to truthfulness; Devil to God; and so on. All this is imposed upon reality, where the mind, in order to exist, separates reality into different ends, as opposites. We must bring them closer through acceptance, and when we do, we will notice the totality of oneness, the reality of the presence in being.

Reality can never be divided into two as each one is but a reflection of the other. Sadness is inherent and intrinsic to happiness; if there is one, the other is bound to be close behind, because in reality they are not two but one. Similarly, to define beauty, we need to relate it to its opposite, ugliness. This dual characteristic is how the mind functions, leading to conflicts and unrest as long as these dualities remain and are not treated as one.

A centered person will not interpret, condemn, choose, justify or judge. He will be focused and accept all that exists without comparing or dissecting.

He will call a rose a rose without relating, comparing or evaluating its beauty, admiring it for what it is, or making it a part of his life, with respect. For him, a rose is a flower, and that is his only reality.

How boring and emotionless it must be, you may think while reading this! Yes, but feelings and emotions are volatile and can be dangerous; they are so deceptive. Sometimes we can be excused for being sensitive rather than overemotional. However, in most cases feelings are attachments and self-centered. We remain attached to those few who we feel belong to us, and we expect the same from them in return. This narrow approach is more sentimental than sensitive. Our reactions to any stimuli should not be related to a few people or what we may expect in return. Our approach expands when we become sensitive to the feelings and condition of all that is around us.

Because sentimentality demands reciprocity, it is more about possessiveness than love. We are so possessed by prejudice, jealousies and expectations, bringing in the duality of love to its opposite – hate, depending on the circumstance.

Existence, in the individual sense, demands duality and life continues with its difficulties. It is up to us to realize and experience reality with consistency and sensitivity towards all, not just special ones.

Allow existence and its natural flow to be full of experience and realization in a simple manner. Opposites are nothing but part of a unified source, separated from their center into two extremes. Do not condemn, judge or defend a point of view; it is a waste of energy to try to find what is right or wrong. What is right for one may be wrong for another. Accept both with respect, grace as part of the total, and keep flowing on in this journey of life, relinquishing the need to compare and judge.

All this leads in one direction – surrender to love. It makes no sense to analyze what is good or bad. We will automatically drop what is not good for us and then see how life starts to change. Acceptance is the center where we neither discriminate nor choose, only exhibit pure love.

The ultimate reality is that God is One.
We all live existentially in that oneness of all.

CHAPTER 16
BEYOND CONSCIOUSNESS

WHEREVER ELSE GOD MAY LIVE, all I know is He lives within me. He is the embodiment of love, compassion and understanding. He may appear in different forms for different people, for He can see the oneness in all. It is only through love that we can bring this oneness to ourselves.

We may possess millions of dollars, but our ego needs to surrender, for it is only then we become aware that we are in fact nothing; our real self is like a drop in the ocean. We do not need to surrender to any superior human being or master but to our own self. Basically it is our ego giving us that identification, which separates us from this oneness of all things.

When the organic body and mind cannot survive without depending on all that is around, why do we keep cutting and dividing, wanting more than what we require? Is it just to satisfy our egos? We keep feeding the ego with thoughts like: 'I am better than and must have more than others'.

In the midst of darkness, light exists. Likewise, in the midst of lies, you find truth. One exists in the presence of the other. It is only the mind, which separates every factor for its own short-term convenience, primarily to exist in duality. Suppose, however, that we combine every duality, and then separation ends, bringing us back to oneness. Dual and non-dual are separated extremes but in one, there is existence in eternal life. Duality brings suffering, non-duality bliss. We need to understand Eastern mysticism so we can use it in the best way for our self-development.

The ancient sages kept repeating, 'neti, neti', (nothing, nothing), for all that exists is just Brahman (energy or spirit). The rest is *Maya* (delusion).

Today, science, after 5000 years, agrees. All that exists in our universe is nothing but energy. To become alive, vibrant and intelligent, it manifests itself in humans, and exhibits dual properties. We need to study and understand the uncertainties of dual and non-dual properties, to know the meaning and purpose of our existence.

As mentioned, in conjunction with this vision of oneness, there is another forgotten Eastern scripture as old as the first (one may find it on the Internet): *Vigyan Bhairav Tantra*, comprising neither dual nor non-dual, but based entirely on oneness, which includes 112 methods of meditation. These methods are applicable as per the requirement of the individual. Here, I discuss some that are general in their function.

The subject of spiritualism begins with self-knowledge and ends with realization. Awareness plays a vital role, ending with non-duality to show that all that exists is not two but one – prevailing, pervading and penetrating all that is in this universe. It further tells us that this is all there is and will be; just let it be and remain in the present now, living from moment to moment.

One needs to be careful, because we can be misled by the contradiction behind duality and non-duality. Moreover, a clear understanding can never come from the mind because the mind, like knowledge and language, has its limitations. It can speak and understand only dualities, whereas non-duality cannot be spoken, only experienced or realized.

No guru or master can give us the awareness, liberation or enlightenment they typically preach.

Attaining knowledge is their job, but when it comes to self-realization, we are our own masters. Only in living existentially, can we experience the self within and realize the similarity that is common to all. Like God, we can only experience.

God is just a method of centring the unified forces within. God and we are one once we realize it. All that is preached by any religion can never make us realize God, only fear Him. We are told repeatedly that if we do this or that, God will do this and that in turn. However, it is how we act and behave, our attitude and character, which reveal the godliness, that lies within us; not from the manipulation of the mind or external experiences. God can only be experienced and realized, in selflessness, compassion, detachment and devotion. When we do not judge or constrict anything in the mind but feel the experience of oneness within, and expand. Duality and non-duality must be centralized and united.

This coming together of opposing properties into one is the ultimate reality in which there is no illusion or delusion. This is the true nature and characteristic of absoluteness. So let it be. But this too, can create confusion since we are required to make every effort in total awareness to bring about this oneness of energy, which has been separated into dualities. Always remember that in our apparent reality, the mind makes us think, not only in *this* but also in *that*, whereas in spirituality there is only the presence of 'This' in totality.

The most beautiful thing in this universe is existence, and in existence, the most beautiful amongst all creatures is the human being. Only human beings have the power to manifest pure, raw energy into intelligence in the form of awareness, passing through thought into intellect and settling in the memory bank of our subconscious as positive or negative consciousness. In animals, we find limited awareness, restricted mainly to food and reproduction.

It is only in indulgence of this conscious knowledge that one can transform, to realize what to accept and what to let go. It is only in action, in how to activate thoughts put into perspective, that one realizes awareness. Therefore, the knowledge passed on by the ancients, is not just to know and understand non-duality, but also to let it be the way it is. Who knows, one of us might have the potential to realize what it is and achieve eternal bliss. For us, the correct path is to learn the methods – how to merge any dual factors, as closely as possible, into their center or oneness, in totality. Otherwise they remain separate and continue to bring sorrow and suffering.

So, how does one awaken to this reality of merging and uniting the dichotomies of life? The spiritual method of centring, as explained, though it may seem simple, is difficult to practise in a life full of complexities. Today, being ordinary, according to me has become more difficult, than to be extraordinary. What a paradox!

Moreover, whatever science, philosophy, psychology or spiritualism may say or preach; each of us has our own unique understanding, knowledge and experience of life. It all depends on our individual power of reasoning, which tells us what we wish to do. So do not impose anything on anybody; let each one utilize his intellect to decide for himself on his own path to comfort, peace and joy. Individuality and uniqueness is the link between life and existence, as represented by the soul.

However reality may be defined, it is an individual's mind that needs to observe, understand and conclude what reality is all about, on his own. Until and unless an individual considers things independently, he cannot come closer to realizing reality than he already has, whatever one may say about non-dual, absolute, oneness, etc.

We also know that these non-dual factors are invisible, ideal and visionary. So those with powers of diction, oration and expression in their preaching or writing, sell dreams to sway weak and dependent people in the direction of their own superior and experienced thoughts, thus taking advantage of their dependency or weakness. The path of non-duality is more about understanding the basis and concept of life rather than venturing on the path of attainment. Only those who dedicate their lives in complete sacrifice, for this completeness, achieve pure consciousness, total awareness or *nirvana*.

Even Buddha was unclear how to achieve *nirvana*, because as long as the mind exists in a human being, there is no way to escape desire – whether to accumulate material things or gain spiritual progress. Therefore, my contention is that by moving these dualities toward their center, there is less friction and disturbance, as both approach oneness. For such a result, understanding both extremes of dualities is necessary.

What is consciousness? It is the inner experiencing of what and who we are. It is the witness within the mind that arrives and exists in duality. Its primary function is to make aware of such awareness, to tell us what and who we are. We are pure energy, pure presence, pure awareness, but unaware of our real existence. It is life. Our individuality starts at birth, struggling with dualities while we exist, and leaves us on our death.

The mind, with its dual characteristics, enjoys playing with us, separating everything in order to discriminate, choose and judge what it desires, until consciousness comes along within its limited space and time to reveal the identity of who we ultimately are. Like a ripple, it comes and quietly goes in the realm of our existence in duality, radiating awareness.

In the list of dualities of our existence, we have God-Devil right on top. God is related to love and the Devil to fear. Both love and fear are pure experiences. We may be possessed by fear or love, but the mind can only describe it as an experience, different in each individual. Love and fear are real experiences, but their descriptions within the mind are unreal as they can only be felt and experienced. Love is the only antidote to fear unless we face fear head on. Bring them closer to their center and they will dissolve into each other to become one. Therefore, we must go beyond consciousness, beyond the mind, not to seek or attain but to act and live toward the direction of non-dual thoughts of oneness. In this way, we reduce duality, inner conflicts, despair, etc., by balancing the two for peace and harmony.

Birth and death are two points at which our energies meet to become one – non-dual and absolute. During fertilization, the sperm meets the egg and becomes one; birth takes place. Similarly, at death, the body decomposes and merges back into mother earth, from which it originated. The interim period, between birth and death, is existence, where the essential oneness, became separated. During fertilization, gender is determined for the continuation of the cycle of life, but there remain traces of each. The male has female hormones and vice versa.

The mind, through its thoughts is programmed to think in a relative manner in order to express what it desires. Even though oneness is a visionary concept, not practical or possible for all, it clearly proves we were and are, one. Inspite of knowing that, we all think, act and exist in reality, only in self-interest, not caring for one another.

Hence, I repeatedly elaborate on a philosophy that goes beyond what consciousness and science can conceive. The ultimate reality, without doubt, lies in the oneness that cannot be denied; though practicality says otherwise, especially in the world in which we live, which is divided into countries, religions, castes, creeds, individual identifications, etc. Let us proceed together on a journey to understand how, in today's world, we can get closer to this oneness, or see whether it is possible to reach anywhere near it. I personally prefer to consider this theory one of 'nearness' rather than 'oneness', in the interests of clarity.

I have created abundant wealth;
I have love that I share with my nearest and dearest;
I have a house in the mountains;
I can go to the beach whenever I like;
I have the whole package, the way I desired;
Yet there is something missing,
as I feel lonely and depressed.
What is it that I still have not found?

CHAPTER 17
ONENESS

KNOWLEDGE OF THE BASIS of oneness originated thousands of years ago, when ancient sages, deep in the forests of India, gave lessons on spiritual living, ranging from meditation, yoga to *karma* and rebirth, declaring all that pervaded this universe to be one; just spirit or energy. This spirit of God was within each of us. Gods of any religion were merely subjects of the self, and truth could only be experienced through faith and freedom rather than under the authority of the mind. These beliefs remain the basis of Buddhism, Taoism, Jainism and spiritualism, to this day.

The essential part of these teachings is that love, truth and reality are attained through experience and realization rather than desire and thought. Remove thoughts of the mind, as these have a tendency to separate things for our benefit only. Bring in the witnessing thoughts of the self; only then will we be able to absorb or comprehend any or all that has been explained and elaborated in this book.

The ancient sages and poets spoke of the concept of the Absolute, of love, eternal life and the ultimate reality of oneness, in the full faith of their consciousness about such ideals, rather than with just the mind. They explained how to experience this unity in existence and not by reading books or intellectually arguing with one another to prove who was right or wrong. Today, however, we want to engineer every faith to our own convenience, and divide and rule Mother Nature for selfish reasons, to receive far more than we require.

Today, thousands of years later, following the expenditure of billions of dollars on researching existence at the subatomic level, scientists have finally discovered that all that exists is nothing but indestructible energy. We now realize that we are not a part of this earth or its unified force; we *are* the earth within a grid of unified consciousness, which reflects us as one. In short, the creator is the creation. The ancients understood the facts we are learning today, about who we are and in what manner we are related to the universe. Through logic and experimentation, science now agrees with what the ancient tenets say: that everything is a part of us; all that we perceive and beyond. We are all indivisible and indestructible, as one.

This unity is the ultimate song of oneness in life. Everything is limitless space, in a timeless cosmos, manifesting as eternal energy that comprises the oneness of all. Greater the cohesion, higher is the equilibrium. More the separation, greater is the distortion and instability. This oneness is both spiritually and scientifically true. However, how can we practice and benefit from it in our existence, where everything is divided and separated?

As mentioned earlier, even our minds are completely separated into extremes of dualities. In fact, the mind cannot function without dualities. Language, of prime importance to man in expressing himself, is also dependent on dualities. To communicate anything and obtain an answer, we need to relate it in the mind and to language. Oneness insists that these dualities have to be superimposed on one another in order to unite into one. This is the vision and reality of oneness, and the ideal situation of perfection.

The same goes for pure consciousness, total awareness, enlightenment, *nirvana*, *moksha*, etc. Ideally, yes, they are perfect as a vision, but in reality, they are very difficult to attain. When a human being has pure consciousness of self or total awareness, he is complete in his totality as one – meaning he becomes God. This is the faith on which Krishna, Buddha and Jesus sacrificed their lives for the betterment of humanity as one, thereby merging into the eternal themselves.

For us, it is important to have this knowledge and, if possible, develop this faith in order to understand the true reality of our being and purpose in life. Extensive research has gone into gaining this clarification of our existence. After all, we are not here just to accumulate, cut and divide, inflate our egos, consider ourselves superior to others, and blindly listen to preachers and follow their experiences.

Our New Age gurus have attempted to make their spiritual philosophies more logical to our engineered minds by merging science with spiritual knowledge. But imagine the simplicity of those ancient times, when there was less logic and technology and more faith and belief.

This unified field of oneness, though impossible today to unite fully and freely, is everywhere and has always been there. It clearly responds to the way we think, feel and act, and is connected to our emotions.

What we need is not science, logic, technology or ego, but a study of the inner self, away from the engineered mind. Individually and collectively, we must change ourselves so we think at a unified field of consciousness. Today, this is tremendously lacking in societies globally. Unless corrected, we are doomed to destroy ourselves by divisions into caste, creed, jealousy, hatred, wars and much else.

I do understand that dualities and opposites in our existence can never meet, for it is in division that one is concerned with superseding the other. If there were no separate positive and negative fields of thinking, bliss would exist all around, making it senseless to write anything on such a subject. Science and spiritualism will no doubt continue to elaborate on this unified force for living as one. In practicality, we should ponder such factors to maintain a certain balance and make our lives more fruitful and fulfilling than they are today.

Therefore, to obtain such balance, we need to observe and understand both extremes of dualities in our existence, and in which direction we lean in each pair of dualities. We then have to find suitable methods to maintain a balance – mentally, physically, emotionally and externally. Everything around us needs balance, especially when we tilt towards greed and self-interest in every field. Mentally, we must reduce the agitations of the mind; emotionally, we must reduce attachments; physically, we must aim for moderation in all we do and consume; and outwardly, we must have respect for Mother Nature, who has given us such abundance.

We have to go beyond both ancient and modern philosophies and theories, beyond any concept of knowledge that the mind can perceive, as none of these have been able to solve any of our basic problems in life. Nor have the preachers who rake in millions trying to give solutions through the mind. None of them have been able to solve or dissolve the pain, suffering and loneliness rampant today due to the separation and non-fulfillment within us. This is all because we are too dependent on our minds and become slaves to what we do.

To learn study and tackle any problem intellectually through the mind is easy. In fact, after coming to know any subject in the mind, we usually begin proclaiming our expertise to others, and try to provide solutions and answers to others' problems. Some succeed very well, depending on their powers of intellect, and spoken and written skills. This happens all too often in the domain of spiritualism, where everyone is desirous of seeking and attaining mental peace.

Few realize that the only way in spiritualism is to live, experience and realize, rather than listen and preach. We have to accept every situation the way it is; live and flow with it; act and improve; to be able to transform and outgrow it. Just desiring, listening, learning and speaking, or improving our knowledge, is not going to provide the desired results.

In spiritual living, it is far better to know through experience and realization. Otherwise the more we know, the greater the complexity in the mind, and more the permutations and combinations with various if's and but's or choosing this or that. Instead, by doing and experiencing, we tend to become different and our vision of life changes. We rely less on the mind and more on intuition, on practicing what we know rather than preaching to everybody all that we profess to know.

What becomes important here is that besides the mind, we may need to restrict the speech and language flowing in our minds. The greater the intellect, the easier it becomes for the mind to convince us and others regarding the dualities of this and that and to discriminate and choose what is in our self-interest, instead of existing in oneness.

While writing these three books and reading the manuscript repeatedly, I realized how the process increased my 'awakening', telling me there is so much more to learn. Every time I read, I would make improvements. The study of spiritualism is never-ending. Self-knowledge, Awareness and Oneness, were the words I attached to each book, but the elaboration required thousands of words. There are bound to be repetitions in the course of various interpretations; so also questions, as the subject continues to be a study-in-progress as further discoveries are made. Each of us must discover our own purpose and meaning in life; never being content with what we hear, read or write; always inspired towards a deeper quest, introspection and intention, despite what we have experienced.

The seeker disappears when he realizes
There is nothing to seek.
In this awareness of nothingness,
The Absolute tells him:
What you seek, you already are.

Chapter 18
Self-Knowledge

Advaita, in ancient scriptures, proclaims there is only one supreme reality: *Brahman* (energy) – infinite, omniscient, omnipresent, omnipotent, and all that in this universe. We cannot subtract or add anything to it, meaning it is present in everything. It transcends all dualities or opposites the mind can conceive or perceive. In short, there is no 'two' in the universe, only 'one'.

What we see is just an optical illusion, a creation of our minds based on our limited perceptions and functioning in the properties of opposites and dualities, called *Maya*, meaning the perceptual world should not be taken as the Ultimate Reality. Even though it has absolute content, by virtue of its characteristics it is subject to constant change. *Maya*, in fact, is not related to the factuality or existence of the world, but only with the awareness of what we see and experience. In reality, we are part of a unified force of consciousness that is eternal and comprises of everything.

Today, this philosophy is no longer mystical or simply a spiritual belief; science agrees that we and the earth, moon and heavens, are one. The body and mind we call our own is temporary, relative and constantly changing, thus making our existence apparent or temporary. The individual body dies along with its identification; what remains is the ultimate force, which was initially responsible for giving the body its individuality and shaping its destiny until its decomposition. The real, intelligent energy, called *atman*, the force behind the body, remains intact and keeps flowing eternally.

For each of us, existence is temporary and unreal; it has no other independent existence, but being part of the whole; Brahmn or energy. Existence, though an illusion, is such a beautiful dream. In my opinion, the purpose of life should be to move towards a balance between the relative and the absolute, and to live this gift of life in the best manner possible –with health, wealth, peace and wisdom. Whatever critics might say, the perceiving self is the only thing that exists. It is our perceiving self, which has coined all these words like Atma, God, Self-realization, or spirit.

Hence, we need to create our own reality in this unreal world; to know about the ultimate reality and so create a balance between oneness and our apparent reality or *Maya*. We need not renounce or give up anything. All we need to do is surrender the ego in order to be strong enough to experience, transform and outgrow all that is not suitable. When we surrender ego, accepting in awareness any situation in its totality, we reach the stage where there is a knowing presence within us. But the mind, at this point, will continue to argue and insist that we choose options according to our own comfort and convenience.

The answer comes naturally, depending on the degree of our personal power. Are we proactive or reactive to such conditions? If proactive, the subsequent step between the subject and object will be spontaneous and intuitive, with little involvement of thought. In the latter case, our thoughts will mull various permutations and combinations of what we should decide, with past and future thoughts destroying the essence of totality.

As in love, if the attraction is spontaneous, in sensitive knowing, the mind proactively accepts this energy in totality. In normal circumstances, however, we consider looks, wealth and personality before falling in love, as a reaction to our spontaneous urges. This becomes a transaction.

However, with spontaneity, experience flows without any prior feelings of accomplishment or regret, transforming in this manner our existential and experiential realization. Without spontaneity, we calculate according to circumstance, space and time, and feel insecure and uncertain; inviting conflicts through the changes, we perceive.

This chapter is based on the Hindu concept, which differentiates between the limited body/mind-self and the limitless Witnessing Self. It claims that awareness is the source, which determines who we are, forming the basis or content of consciousness. This Essential Self exercises a path of liberation during its existence in the various cycles of birth and death until it attains moksha. Meaning there is an endless series of births and deaths; through karma, dharma and samsara, to attain moksha or freedom. On achieving liberation, the self-consciousness is no longer identified with the 'conventional self' but is pure consciousness or total awareness.

It is interesting to note here that most spiritual literatures today emphasize Consciousness and Self-realization in pure consciousness rather than its source, Awareness. In the external world, 'who we are' is of prime importance, but in spiritualism, 'what we are' is given relevance. In awareness, the individual sees the world permeated by particles of total awareness as one Absolute Reality. In other words, when we awaken from our ignorance, to know about the source of the Real Self, the world starts to exist in its Ultimate Reality.

Ultimate reality says we are one; living in oneness is bliss, and all that pervades is one single, unified force. Undoubtedly, this fact should be our ultimate goal. As for me, living in this physical world of Maya, I still need to cover a lot of ground before I can reach anywhere near that point. I need to abandon my body, mind and dual existence to develop my awareness to reach that level of purity and totality in oneness. We all know that until we sacrifice ourselves to the universe in totality, it is impossible to reach anywhere close to pure consciousness and total awareness. What then can we do?

As explained earlier, despite being complete, until we realize this ultimate reality, we remain unfulfilled. We will need to go through the cycle of birth and death repeatedly until we reach salvation. Until then, our innermost, intelligent energy will keep manifesting in an apparent manner, making us exist in dualities or opposites, causing pleasure and pain, happiness and sorrow; keeping us always wanting and dejected in life. Therefore, both dualities and opposites, which are unfortunately a part of us, need to be tamed in the mind, even if we cannot reach the ultimate point. For this, we will be undertaking many centring methods in an effort to bring each duality as close as possible to its meeting point, the center from which it has been separated. This is not so we can be God, but to seek peace, harmony and tranquility; not by renouncing, but by living in comfort and totality.

If positive and negative are treated as equal, with respect, in surrender, acceptance and totality, are we not bound to benefit from such unison? We would be more composed and balanced. Here, surrender in no way means giving up our freedom; what it stands for is giving up the inner arguments and conflicts within, and surrendering the ego in favor of reality. For reality is simply being present, moment-to-moment, alert and aware, accepting, facing whatever the situation, may be, as it exists before us.

Our attitude in life thus becomes centered and focused existence rather than emotionally in any situation. What we need to remember here is that dualities or opposites are a part of a complete whole, though they remain separated in our minds in order for us to exist, discriminate and choose; to be different from all other creatures, who do not have this unique characteristic. We are specialized creatures; our energies separate in dual properties for us to experience good and bad. How we individually do so is the subject under discussion. This point may have been repeated a number of times, but is necessary to drive home the depth of the mystery which we are faced with.

Separation is further aggravated when we notice that many of us, in spite of possessing an abundance of wealth, health, personal love and comforts, are still not fulfilled. There is disturbance, agony and loneliness, creating emptiness. This happens when the body and mind are not aligned with the spirit; clearly signifying the importance and need to understand spiritualism in our lives. In fact, the same misalignment becomes the cause as well as symptom of many ailments, leading to diseases of both mind and body. Doctors refer to this as stress; spiritualism refers to it as not being in rhythm with our real self.

The more self-centered we are, the more our thoughts will control us. They will revolve around 'I', thinking it separate and superior to others, leading us to feelings of happiness when we get what we want, or feelings of fear, anxiety and suffering when we do not. The relationship exists only between our identity and wants. Remove one and the other disappears.

In this knowledge, thoughts come and go but awareness remains in the subconscious as memory, as a factor in knowing. We call this factor consciousness. Always remember that the substance of any thought, from the past or present, is the sum total of our awareness, but awareness is independent of both. Like a gold ornament that is melted down or the wave in an ocean that comes and goes, the gold and the ocean remain, independent of their previous apparent existence, yet real, like awareness.

Between one thought and another, there is a gap, when the mind is silent – in which our being or awareness comes to make us conscious of what is happening. Everything we perceive is thought, but that is not what we are. We are the being existing in the knowing presence of the mind called awareness; which, functioning in separation or duality becomes a part of it. Combined at the center, dualities become one. The thinking mind cannot comprehend the real us as the aware being. This is where self-knowledge, self-awareness and self-experience count; where a real guru or master is required. Learn, understand and know from such a person, who will teach based on his own experience and not from a book.

The idea of being spiritually awakened is a fallacy unless we live moment to moment, in pure knowledge, with the knowing presence of awareness of who we are. Like many others, we may think, or let the ego dictate, that we have reached that stage. However, on true self-examination, our awareness will tell us whether we are still the victim of wants, doubts and bondage because of our self-identity, or not.

This is why the mind and science, both of which cannot capture truth in its absoluteness (being accustomed to perceive only what is tangible), are unable to know we are that invisible, knowing presence or awareness. All else just comes and goes. It is, in fact, simple: either we are the mind through thought, which keeps changing from this to that; or we are awareness. Having reached this far, we should be able to answer that question for ourselves.

Many people may favor being what they are, in body and mind, with their own self-identity and see them selves as complete, presuming this to be their reality. This is what the mind lives for – not to question beyond. If the intellect were convinced of this notion, it would be futile to say otherwise. It may then be better to live such a life, dancing to the tune that suits one the best. Ultimately, we are our own masters.

However, if we are concerned inwardly about discovering the realities of life, then Self-knowledge is essential. We will want answers to questions like:

'How can the concept of 'I' be real if it is changing all the time?' 'Are the constant changes in life responsible for my anxiety, fear, sadness and suffering?' If, under so many pressures we begin taking antidepressants, would it not be wiser to understand the real, unchanging self hiding within, in ignorance; and accept this knowing awareness as the real Self?

When the knower knows the known,
knowing disappears. When there is no desire, the knower
knows without knowing.

CHAPTER 19
SUBLIME AWARENESS

WE NEED TO BE IN LOVE with what we are doing; this way, we do what we love, without worrying about what is good or bad. There should be no past or future to disturb us in what we are doing. Our intuition, combined with past awareness, the subconscious, our inherent attitude, and knowledge of the subject at hand, will direct us in what we are doing. Our pure presence in the moment is required for fresh awareness to enter and enlighten the creativity within us. We must be aware of the present and concentrate on what we are doing. In this way, we will automatically reject what we do not approve of.

This is not to negate the mind in any manner. The mind is undoubtedly our most valuable instrument. But what we need to understand though, is that the mind is so powerful that it overpowers and takes control without our realizing it. Concentrating on the present, moment to moment, and being absorbed in what we are doing, balances the mind. Otherwise, its complex thoughts about the past, present and future prevent us from considering what is at hand – we become emotional and are led astray by many other factors.

Creative results are obtained only when the mind is centered, away from past and future thoughts, and brought into the present to focus on what we are doing. This way, the mind is attuned to what we are doing, and under our command; making us the masters.

Achieving this may seem difficult, but the mind does so whenever we come up with something creative – in spontaneous awareness of our presence, where the focus is purely on the subject rather than its outcome. The trouble is, the conscious mind, constantly under siege by emotions and selfishness, creates a dark shadow, disturbing the purity of its actions, so that it can analyze and calculate rather than focus on the subject at hand.

To express this philosophically or spiritually, I would say one needs to go beyond the mind and consciousness to become absorbed totally in the present moment, aware and alert, with nothing to hinder it; in total surrender of the ego; in acceptance. In such cases, when the doer is doing, he and his mind disappear; what remains is the unison of action, with no identification to the individual. At this stage, creativity flourishes and opposites start drawing closer to where there is no positive or negative, centring on the point of origin – oneness.

Even though this has been repeated time and again, the intention here is to drive home the essence of this message deeply; which otherwise might be taken lightly due to its simplicity. The mind needs to be transformed, for the mind is always wanting and in doubt, which never ceases. How long can we remain in such a state of mind – always desirous, doubting, suspicious, anxious, going from the past into the future, never satisfied, wanting more and more?

In youth, fair enough, the mind should desire more and more; only then can we expect to get somewhere in life. But as knowledge increases, and basic ambitions are achieved, we arrive at a crossroads where we ask: 'Why am I still unhappy? What is it that I really want?' That is the period in life when we need to contemplate, turn inward, silence the mind, and awaken from the separation that is the cause of all misery. The answer lies in finding what we need to do to bring alignment and harmony into living each day.

We have to be wary of the mind debating and questioning everything endlessly. That is the reason for its tremendous material success. Give the mind anything to think about and it will dissect it into many thoughts. So be careful of the mind – never let it become the master. It should be used more for the external requirements of food, clothing, shelter and comforts. When it comes to understanding the self and going inward for self-development, it is necessary to quieten or silence the mind, allowing it to flow with love, surrender and acceptance.

The whole process is not at all complicated; in fact, it is so simple that preachers may find it difficult to communicate. Because our originality and individuality are retained, we need not depend on or be impressed by, the experience and greatness of any other mind, for we are no longer weak.

A certain strength within us tells us we are our own masters. Every act requires the essence of meditation and concentration with alertness and totality. There is no conflict in the mind because it has been silenced. Through internal questioning, we become contemplative and creative. We no longer question, thinking: What is there for me? Why should I make any effort? As we continue with our existence, we become more sensitive toward others and more experienced in the results of our actions.

Note that 'not using the mind' or 'going beyond' it, are metaphors or figures of speech, not to be taken literally. They are used to emphasize that the mind (voluntary or conscious), should be used only as an instrument (like other parts of the body), as and when required. Surprisingly, it is the voluntary or conscious mind that is the culprit behind our anxieties. Spiritually, the subconscious mind plays an important role, as our attitudes originate here. If the two are not in harmony, we have a big problem.

The subconscious and unconscious are autonomous and involuntary. This is where our previous awareness or consciousness goes and settles as memory – for that is what we are, for good or bad. The job of the mind is to know and memorize; everything else originates from here. The unconscious mind becomes active when the conscious part goes to sleep. Under normal circumstances, it keeps working during sleep to bring forth answers. When our conscious part awakens, it accesses the answers through memory. If the subconscious is in accord with our actions, thoughts from the conscious mind remain stable and at peace. (Of course, these are views and opinions, which may or may not align with the scientific theory on this subject.)

Therefore, spirituality demands we enter the no-mind zone. We know the mind and existence are impossible without thoughts. The no-mind zone is where we train the mind meditatively, using thoughts to tune the conscious and the subconscious to the present moment, from one moment to the next, rather than letting them get mixed up with past and future thoughts, as they usually do. In this way, the intellect will be less emotional; focused and constructive, in performing the job at hand. It will also be simpler and more creative rather than separated; in conflict with our emotions and wants.

The 'no-mind zone' is the energy-field prior to the formation of thought. It is the zone of silent stillness from where thoughts arise. The ego-mind is under the impression that if it stops thinking or feeling, the mind will die. Therefore, it treasures the desire to think and relentlessly relies on it. The no-mind zone demands to bypass thoughts when we relax the mind, breathe deeply and focus on what is being witnessed. We notice the approach of closeness between the witness and the observer. We are then aware of what is being witnessed and the mind is bypassed.

The sixth sense is awakened, the sense of the Real Self moves from content (thoughts), to context (Awareness), and divine wisdom flows. Remember that the loss of thoughts in no way results in a void or nothingness, as often claimed. The Self is always fully aware of its presence as the Ultimate Reality, which in no way can be considered a void or nothingness. Instead, it is the awareness of all that exists. Knowing and 'allness' simply replaces everything in the mind through observance. This is what meditation, introspection and contemplation is about. The difference is that one's awareness is still; it does not make any comment within the mind. Nothing is everything. It is only when we are nothing that 'allness' exists. One is free of emotions and external perceptions are replaced by awareness.

The mind is thus unbiased and free; our greed and desires are unable to suppress the pure functioning of this beautiful machine. This is the stage I wish for you to transcend – to reach the point at which there is silence and subtlety, balance and serenity. Spiritual living is as difficult as walking a tightrope. On a rope stretched tightly from both ends, we have to be cautious not to tilt to any side, and maintain our balance and poise. In the same way, in life, we need to balance good and bad, God and the Devil, within us, drawing them closer towards the center. Balance depends on desires at one end and reality on the other, with us poised on that tightrope holding the pole of dichotomies; both ends are essential. How we manage this balance is the art of spiritual living.

Spiritualism today is usually in the form of knowledge. There are innumerable books and preachers, doing business as usual, each branding himself in a different style. However, despite all that knowledge, each of us remains deeply involved in amassing and accumulating as much as we can, living in an illusion of materialism, with the dream that it will give us happiness and peace. We keep cheating and dividing, making the world messy, ugly and confused. This is the reason we need to understand the vision of oneness, which has been shattered and broken into pieces. All we are required to do is to understand the concept and play our part subconsciously, thus bringing the mind into balance and closer to unity.

Just as the sun is not aware of its light,
Or the moon of its beauty, you do not know your centre:
I am That.

CHAPTER 20
MECHANICS OF CENTRING

EVERYTHING IN LIFE MOVES in cycles or circles, whether it is birth, death or the weather. Each starts from a certain point and comes back to that same point. The periphery of each cycle determines its mechanism, but the outcome is governed by its center, which is the conglomeration of anything and should always be taken seriously. Similarly, in the cycle of birth and death, we conjoin as one in the sexual act while the sperm and egg fertilize as one, complete in all respects. It then separates, as per its chromosomes, into gender. At the end of life it returns to where it came from, to once again conjoin with the universal energy; only to repeat the cycle again and again; seeking evolution and fulfilment during the period of each life cycle.

Centring the various energies in our existence is a process of merging our scattered physical, mental, social, emotional and financial energies into our core self, through experiential realization in forming our consciousness. This center determines the soul of awareness signifying who you are.

When we are not in consonance with our center and submerged more in our mind, we have anxiety and fear. The process of centring provides methods, revealing that our body and mind due to desires in ego and self-interest needs to consistently attune. We are required to introspect, contemplate, meditate and reconcile in order to integrate the scattered and separated energies to the wholeness of what and who we are.

When you are centered, you begin to move more inwards, becoming sensitive and aware of the dualities in opposites, merging them with the awareness of your presence rather than only being restricted to the external perceptual thoughts of the mind. Your inner witness perceiving through consciousness expands.

To me, whenever I am hyper-active, agitated, worried or anxious, I try to centralize my energies by reading through the pages of a spiritual book, going for a walk or meditating in awareness by surrendering my ego to accept that situation in neutrality. This way, I reduce the resistance to whatever is making me anxious.

Kindly remember, any behavior or habit, which takes us away from our center, should be avoided; any sort of excessive addictions, judging others, gossiping about others, negatively speaking behind other's back etc.

Most of us, if we are truthful, will agree that we are off-centered, mainly because of ignorance. Since childhood, we are conditioned into imitating whatever is taught to us, in believing on other's beliefs and experiences to follow them blindly in our egoistic desires in attachments and accumulations.

This creates an attitude of separateness in mental constrictions and muscular contractions leading to anxiety and tensions. To overcome such adverse situations, we should contemplate and introspect in order to know your own-self and become aware. Then try to attune your consciousness towards that awakening and without any suppression or regression, surrender, accept and act in accordance to that situation. You will notice, most of your drawbacks go back to your childhood, the way you have been brought up.

The secret of life is to make an effort, intentionally or otherwise, to bring these extremes towards their center, where they belong. The closer we can bring them, the better our life will be. This is how we can change the course of our destiny – through various methods of centring. Destiny, as commonly believed, is not fixed or unchallengeable. There is no doubt that success lies with the person who can master his own mind and destiny.

Remember, consciousness is what we are and mind is the activity that unfolds the consciousness.

Mind, by virtue of its design to think in desire and separation, is unable to differentiate truth from its falsehood. Mind is like the processor in a computer, it plays back only what has been programmed into it - until awareness emerges to make the mind conscious of itself.

With a strong attitude of surrender, acceptance and humility, we centralize the self to the stage where ego is replaced with compassion, desire with selflessness, and accumulations with detachment. This is possible only with the power of intention, where the evolution of the mind centralizes life into a prayer of supplication and surrender. This is the reason spiritual progress and its intention can never be through on artificial means. It is through this spiritual centring or intention that the possibility of rising in consciousness can be converted from probability to actuality.

The secret lies in the art of managing the mind, which is designed to function in dualities. However, we have the power and awareness to break this rule. Bring such dualities away from their extremes, back towards their center, as close as possible, and watch the results. This center is the core of our pure consciousness, the absolute energy declared by science and spiritualism as the unified force of consciousness – oneness.

The splendor of our being as creator and creation, as absolute or ultimate reality, has meaning only if we are ready to accept this fact – that we are one and not two. This is based on the theory that any formation is always part of a greater design, a larger system, which itself belongs to another greater one, unto infinity.

I asked: 'Who is God?' Even though I was taught that God was within me and I was God; since He is omnipresent, omnipotent and omniscient, it sounded absurd and incomplete. In spiritualism I learned the same truth but in a simpler manner. The mind and body, that is physical matter, decomposes and dissolves back into Mother Nature, from which it originated. Intelligent energy, on the other hand, being indestructible and indivisible, transmigrates to start another cycle of birth and death.

In this way, the cycle of birth and death continues in the travelling of intelligent energy from one birth to another, until it reaches a body that is selfless, and there is no separation in the mind because it is fulfilled, pure and loving; accepting the wholeness all around. He embodies the pure consciousness in total awareness. Such a person fulfils his completeness and lives eternally. Shining examples are Christ, Buddha, Krishna and a few others; they realized enlightenment to become God themselves and live forever.

Therefore, instead of swinging from one extreme of any duality to the other, practice the art of centring, learning not to lean to any side. For this, we must strengthen certain characteristics in ourselves; and experiences that which draws us towards the center, where we really belong; respectful and caring of the awareness, which takes us further on the spiritual journey. The centring methods given in the next chapter are based on meditative techniques, focus, concentration, discipline and dedication, and are to be practiced with awareness. Some of these have been mentioned in Books I and II, but here I have gone into more detail.

Only then, can we surrender, accept, outgrow and transform ourselves from the dualities of our existence. Balance, poise, alertness, choicelessness, intuitiveness, spontaneity and sensitivity are characteristics of those who truly wish to undertake this journey as their life's purpose.

Chapter 21
Methods of Centring

LISTENING: Our minds, as we know, chatter all the time; they rattle on excessively with what we know, so that others will listen to us. This makes us happy. However, we need to remember that the mind can only exist in the past and make projections about the future. Listening, on the other hand, brings us into the present, the center, where, for that moment, the mind's chatter ceases. It helps in developing awareness and allowing a certain discipline.

We need not give advice or lecture all the time; we must control our egos and listen. Many learned people become irritated when they have to listen to someone else. However, the fact is that our learning process reduces if we do not know how to listen. Seemingly simple, it is difficult to listen attentively.

We need to set aside our own mind while listening; and concentrate; making listening a meditative aspect of life. In listening, do not analyze or start to discriminate between what is good or bad. Just be in the center, with the speaker and the subject, and let awareness evolve through listening.

Silence: Silence is pure splendor and absolute. It is sound that is dual; it needs a source as transmitter and a receiver to hear. Between any two sounds, there is a gap of silence, in order to define that sound. Sound, on further expansion, is expressed through words and language, which also belongs to the dual category.

Sound can never possess the property of absorption; it mainly creates noise and disturbance. It keeps being detached from its center into high or low pitches, losing its identity until it reaches back into silence, to start a new note. Sound represents discrimination, desire and demand. Whenever we are disturbed, we notice silence drawing closer to us. Silence ultimately resolves sound into unity and oneness.

Silence, quietude or stillness, make us realize who we really are. Silence the mind, make it quiet; stop the chain of thoughts. At that moment, we enter into the present, either in full concentration, or at least begin going inward, away from all the restless chattering of thoughts, the blaring of the TV, beeping of mobile phones, etc.

Learning how to still the mind and travel inward is popular these days; it is the modern anti-anxiety medication. From New York to New Delhi, the practice of searching for inner peace has become big business, where *vaastu*, feng shui, New Age gurus, astrologers, shrinks, yoga teachers – are all teaching ways and means of stilling the mind, guiding us from meditation to gentle stretching, from chanting mantras to quietude, from breathing exercises to the intricacies of yogic practice.

The fact is we are all in a hurry. Our thoughts are driving us mad or bringing turmoil into our lives because they are driven by greed and fear. Greed tells us there is no time to lose, while fear tells us we may lose what we are clutching at. We are running from everyday pressures, making our lives more complex, trying to accumulate too much in too short a time, eventually breaking down physically and mentally, restless and diseased, not realizing how slowly and steadily nature moves, while achieving everything.

Quietude is the beginning of the journey toward inner freedom and peace. In fact, meditation involves complete stillness of the mind. In stillness, the mind quietens and becomes introspective, and we then indulge in the present moment. We become fully aware in the consciousness of our being and relax into ourselves. When this happens, we go with the flow of the present rather than hurrying along in the age of technology and digitalization, trying to achieve maximum productivity.

Both extremes are relevant to understanding the wholeness of our oneness. Notice how everything in the universe happens silently, so peacefully, without any contradictions – like the solar system functioning in such beauty, telling us that things happen in nature in spite of us, not because of us. In the same way, sounds, words, language, thoughts and the mind have brought us to where we are today. Applying this centring method, knowing both extremes, becomes even more interesting.

Laughter: We have all read the lovely phrase in *Reader's Digest*: 'Laughter is the best medicine'. Believe it or not, if a patient smiles and laughs, the doctor may not need to prescribe medication. Laughter is the strongest curative.

I was born into a very religious family and gradually drew away from it, the reason: there was no humor or laughter in my family's religion. It seemed sullen, serious and depressing at times. This may be why most of us spend very little time in temples and churches. It is just too serious, devoid of enjoyment, laughter, fun and frolic.

Today, when I see people laughing, many do so under the influence of alcohol, trying to calm their anxious nerves; or they laugh artificially. Laughter needs nothing other than the intelligence to understand wit. Seriousness, on the other hand, is accepted as sacred, respected and honored. Few realize that laughter dissolves seriousness, bringing back the child in us, taking us back in time, and deflating our ego. When we stop laughing, we revert to the devious, thinking mind. In laughter there is just us, glowing and egoless.

APPRECIATION: Real pleasure, we are told, comes from unconditional love. We are so concerned about our own selves and our near and dear ones, that we get more pleasure in others appreciating us than from thinking about them. When someone else is appreciated in our presence, it is usual to experience jealousy.

The challenge in life lies in a neutral attitude, in being able to transmit positive vibrations of appreciation – not only to those close to us, but even to those who may wish us harm. In this way, our attitudes toward life become centered, away from any one extreme.

ACCUMULATION: The basic nature of the mind is to accumulate. It starts with education, when we are taught to gather and excel. The journey begins with collecting knowledge, material things, spiritual data, etc. Here, emotion is the dominant factor; our purpose is to enhance the quality of our lives.

The human mind formulates to progress and enlarge only through accumulation. However, that turns into greed, desire and constant dissatisfaction, which leads to feelings of insecurity, loneliness, grief, and eventually sadness. The paradox is that the more we have, the more insecure we feel.

Then a stage comes when our accumulated emotions and thoughts wish to be liberated in awareness. Then we want to distance ourselves from what we feel and desire; we want our energies to overcome limitations and bonds, and flow into a life, which is part of nature; not just snatch and accumulate what we can.

Awareness of the other extreme takes us to the practice of giving, loving and selflessness; to becoming concerned not only with oneself but with humanity at large. The best method I have found is to practice moderation, in every factor of life. Desires will always be there, but try to limit oneself; anything in excess becomes counterproductive and harmful. Think and work for oneself; then think for others, family and friends; that is how goodness and oneness originates.

Selflessness: This is probably the toughest. The goodness of which lies behind it is pure godliness. We live in a dualistic world, in which the mind is designed to function for self-interest; hence selflessness seems to be asking for too much. Nevertheless, all enlightened and realized souls have this in common: they were all selfless and became one with God.

This remains more of a vision for most of us who exist and remain separated since we are only about ourselves. In fact, selflessness and selfishness are two sides of the same coin, the center of which is oneness. However, so what if oneness is a vision? By going deep into thoughts on this subject, we will realize its significance. Envy, jealousy, hatred and terrorism all happen due to the lack of oneness in our world.

Today, due to globalization, economies and markets are reaching every corner of the world. What we see is every individual, society and country are out to grab benefits and pull others down. If we can realize how much we are moving toward the extreme of selfishness, we may be able to consider the efficacy of sharing the abundance of everything nature offers.

What I am saying is that we are now at one extreme; why not reduce this gap and make the effort to give selflessly, with no expectations, without inflating our egos, because we are givers? Nature and oneness has beautifully provided for us. If we start giving selflessly, with no personal intentions, we are bound to receive from sources all around us, when we least expect it.

This is the highest centring method one may apply at one's own will and capacity. A word of caution though: keep in mind that in giving, the ego can become inflated, gradually bringing us down to where we started from. Even without letting anyone know we have given, it still inflates the ego. One should be selfless – without motivation or action prompted by the mind; but naturally, with a feeling of love and compassion. This by itself is meditation.

Therefore, higher our acts of selflessness, greater will be the oneness. We will be able to see in others the same, common, single self – the unified force of consciousness, which exists in continuum, making us all interrelated, interdependent and interconnected. As the *Bible* says: *Love thy neighbor as thyself.* Learn the art of selfless action; trying to develop such an attitude; it will reduce the ego and bring us closer to oneness, the center at which we can reduce the other extreme of selfishness.

FEARLESSNESS: We are told humans have two primal or basic emotions: love and fear.

Fear is the driving force to survive; love enables us to thrive. The two have been the foundations of human history. Fear is an emotion we have always had and will have. In fact, a large part of our brain comprises areas dedicated to instinctive fear.

Fear originates as a self-preservation instinct in animals. Even now, in humans, when faced with threats to survival, fear emanates from the endocrine glands through hormones, inducing increased heart rate, high blood pressure, insomnia, etc. These physical symptoms serve to reinforce the feelings, creating anxiety and playing havoc with our minds and bodies; to the extent that abstract matters like higher interest rates, business losses, losing jobs, disapproval of bosses or spouses, can affect our lives.

Fear has many faces and comes in many guises, as anger, perfectionism, pessimism, anxiety, depression, insecurity, feelings of isolation; often morphing into one after the other, but rarely declaring itself. Fear, when it starts emerging in the brain, travels into the body and begins to poison every part it touches, making it the strongest negative emotion known to humankind.

Fearlessness does not mean we have been able to eliminate fear; it means going beyond it. Fear, in fact, needs to be acknowledged and accepted. We must realize fear; only then can we counter it head-on. Being fearless and loving can take us toward godliness, for love is the only antidote to fear; it dissolves fear. If love is missing, the same fearlessness can overreact and turn into a powerful devil. The *Upanishads* say: *Fearlessness is God.* It guards the mind from all weaknesses.

COMPASSION: Compassion is that awareness of the oneness, I keep talking about. It is the ultimate emotion through which a person succeeds in his journey toward fulfilment. Selflessness and compassion go hand in hand. All enlightened souls have had compassion as their main embodiment of communion with others. Compassion is the indication of the maturity of our emotions. If we practice it sincerely, it can lead to self-fulfillment.

On one extreme, we have sorrow, misery and an attitude of indifference; on the other, there is empathy and compassion. For self-development, it is necessary to consider humility and selflessness as major components of equanimity. The journey begins with love, fearlessness and selflessness, to compassion as the ideal path to ultimate oneness.

The following four centring methods are means by which we can balance our lives and give back to society, in return for the many things we receive.

ACCEPTANCE: Whatever the present moment may contain, accept it, as this will take us to a deeper level, an inner state, away from the mind's judgment of good and bad. Always work with, not against it, as it will decrease the gap between one extreme and another. Accept both extremes of duality with equal respect and grace. Only then can we act neutrally in whatever situation we find ourselves. Accepting the unacceptable is the greatest achievement.

Acceptance means we accommodate people, situations, circumstances and events as they occur, accepting the presence of every moment as it should be, because the whole universe is the way it is; just this. This moment, the one we are experiencing right now, is a bundle of moments we have experienced in the past; only it gets better and wiser. In struggling against the present moment, we actually struggle against the universe.

Acceptance in this context does not mean giving up or resigning, it is a gesture of humility, signifying that there is always more to a situation than our own small perspective. It is merely willingness to agree that there exists a larger plan than what we can perceive with our senses.

This means we should accept things as they are and not as we wish them to be. Whenever there is a stimulus, we are bound to respond. In the gap – the time between a stimulus and response – we have choice. This choice can be a reaction originating from our feelings, or acceptance of the moment in flow with the stimulus, in proactive mode. The latter allows us to tackle stimulus with a creative response and turn every situation into an opportunity.

Aloneness: The word 'loneliness' suggests sadness, sorrow and being lonesome, whereas 'aloneness' stands for strength and the grit to be by yourself, solely and exclusively. Aloneness is the rare pleasure few of us learn to enjoy, and it does not at all mean we are lonely. In fact, it shows that we have the ability to be on our own and not depend on others.

Many of us are uncomfortable with ourselves and therefore reluctant to be alone, constantly craving company. By being dependent on others, we tend to falter when we are confronted with emergencies. It overshadows our individuality, highlighting our weakness; making us realize how little we know about our own self and inner strength.

Solitude and isolation should be practiced as much as one desires meditation. This particular strength, through being alone, confident and calm, ensures we are there for ourselves when we are forlorn or when desolation stalks us. Remember that aloneness is not being lonely, nor is solitude running away from others. In fact, it is when we can love our own company.

By being with oneself, one has the opportunity to analyze one's thoughts, contemplate, and introspect, away from outer and inner disturbances, and detoxify the mind. Further, it provides a tool for practicing meditation, prayer or other spiritual exercises. Solitude does not mean withdrawing from society or not interacting with other people. In fact, it helps us grow in society, yet also to be away from it; in the same way, a lotus flower blooms among weeds without being affected by anything around it.

Love: Love is the emotion necessary for internal purification. It can dissolve all things negative.

Throughout history, people have believed that love comes from the heart rather than the mind. The heart and brain, in order to function smoothly and in balance, have to be constantly in dialogue with one another. With every emotion, we notice our heart rate changing, showing the two are interconnected in the nervous systems.

Love has two connotations; one is relative – a relationship between two human beings, signifying expectations, possessiveness, attachments, desires, demands and jealousy, etc.; hatred as it's opposite.

The other form of love is absolute: pure and serene, an antidote to everything negative the mind can perceive or conceive of.

Love, in either form, besides the fulfilment it confers, is also the supreme healing power. The power to erase and neutralize all negativity makes this energy paramount and divine. Love, in its non-dual property, demands complete sacrifice. Then it remains eternal. On the other hand, when expectations arise from love, and those desires are unfulfilled, it can lead to hurt, contempt, turning love into its duality – hate. We need to accept both, the dual and non-dual and practice both, as we cannot have one without the other, keeping the mind uninvolved as far as possible. When pure and pristine love flows, it dissolves all the negativity that it touches.

Even when there is an abundance of love all around, it moves very slowly. Its opposite, fear, moves quickly. For example, it may take years to gather a group of people who think and feel about love as we do, but a group can be gathered in an instant if we express hatred for any person, group or society.

Love is the presence of truth and compassion, whereas hate thrives on greed and fear. While the spirit thrives on love, the mind thrives on greed and jealousy. On one extreme, we have absolute love in oneness; on the other, hurt and hatred, separating one from the other. What better centring method can there be than knowing this, so we can work to reduce the gap between dualities and fulfil our purpose in life?

In life, we need both logic and love. Logic is a pure manifestation of the mind, while love is the energy beyond the mind and thoughts. Love is spontaneous, an experience of the now. When the mind captures it to understand and narrate that experience, it no longer remains the same. Love is converted into thoughts and feelings, creating expectations, conditions, possessiveness, preferences, jealousies, etc.

Lust and possessiveness are often mistaken by the mind for love. The mind confuses love after it experiences it, and love no longer remains in its totality. It is separated into mixed feelings and thoughts of this and that. Love can never be taught, described or narrated by the mind. The beauty of love is that it is the only energy that fulfils in being given and received. Love has no ego and is unconditional. It is neither related to the heart, emotions or mind, for it is pure experiential energy. Do not try to pursue love. It is there within us, without our knowing, it will flow spontaneously in pure giving, whether for an individual in passion or for togetherness in compassion. It can only be experienced in silence, not through words.

Spiritualism says love between two cannot exist. Love needs sensitivity and compassion to all; otherwise, it weakens and separates into duality. Love, in such cases is bound to be diluted, by conditions, expectations, preferences and jealousies; calculated by the mind for its own satisfaction.

Love is the spontaneous energy of spirit that is happening in the now, flowing on with no expectations or conditions. The greater its purity, the more we move towards spiritual love in godliness. This is why in spiritualism there is only one and not two.

We try to connect our hearts with love through our minds, though the heart is a physical organ. When we use words in trying to speak from the heart in a poetic manner, we call it emotion. However, these are only thoughts in motion. Emotions too, though related to the heart, originate and settle in the mind, demanding something or the other in return. Thus, even though emotions are connected to the heart, they are present in the mind rather than the physical organ of the heart.

Always remember: love is neither a property nor a characteristic of the mind or heart. Love is God. It is the presence of being in the now; the experience of becoming aware and always wanting to give, not take.

Love is supreme energy.

ACKNOWLEDGEMENTS

I am indebted to the following people:

Friends and family members, who encouraged me at every step, indulging me during my lengthy monologues on the subject of Spirituality. Their invaluable critiques helped me tide over doubts and rough stages during the writing process;

My Editors, for improving form and content, and patiently re-reading drafts of the manuscript;

To my wife Komilla Kumar, thank you for your patience, love, support and inspiration.

To my children, Nadisha Gulati and Shreeya Kumar Bhola, who will always be my creative force.

Finally, I dedicate this in memory of my parents, my greatest inspiration, for making me who I am today.

www.ingramcontent.com/pod-product-compliance
Lightning Source LLC
Chambersburg PA
CBHW031125090426
42738CB00008B/975